# Delivering Inclusive and Impactful Instruction

*Universal Design for Learning in Higher Education*

## Kevin L. Merry

Bulk discounts available: For details, email *publishing@cast.org* or visit *www.castpublishing.org*.

Copyright © 2024 by CAST, Inc. All rights reserved.

No part of this publication may be reproduced or transmitted in any form or by any means, electronic or mechanical, including photocopy, recording, or any information storage and retrieval systems, without permission in writing from the publisher.

Library of Congress Control Number: 2023910779

Paperback ISBN 978-1-943085-04-0
Ebook ISBN 978-1-943085-05-7

Published by:
CAST Professional Publishing
an imprint of CAST, Inc.
Lynnfield, Massachusetts, USA

Cover and interior design by Happenstance Type-O-Rama
Printed in the United States of America

*For Malc and Linda.*
*Without you, I wouldn't be here.*

# Contents

*Preface* . . . . . . . . . . . . . . . . . . . . . . . . . . . *vii*

**PART I**   UDL AND MODERN HIGHER EDUCATION

   1  *The Changing Nature of Higher Education* . . . . . . . 3
   2  *Universal Design for Learning* . . . . . . . . . . . . . 7
   3  *Learner Variability* . . . . . . . . . . . . . . . . . . 17

**PART II**   UNDERLYING PRINCIPLES

   4  *The Meaning of Mastery* . . . . . . . . . . . . . . . . 35
   5  *Roadmap for Teaching* . . . . . . . . . . . . . . . . . 41
   6  *What We've Always Done* . . . . . . . . . . . . . . . . 51
   7  *The Cheese Sandwich* . . . . . . . . . . . . . . . . . 55
   8  *The Cheese Sandwich and How People Learn* . . . . . . . 77

**PART III**   DESIGNING FOR MASTERY

   9  *Goal-Directed Learning* . . . . . . . . . . . . . . . . 83
 10  *Learning Activities* . . . . . . . . . . . . . . . . . 91

**11** Demonstrating Understanding . . . . . . . . . . . . 101
**12** The Criticality of Feedback . . . . . . . . . . . 111
**13** A Word on Technology . . . . . . . . . . . . . 119

## PART IV   MASTERY IN ACTION

**14** Putting It All Together . . . . . . . . . . . . . 139
**15** Evaluating Learning and Teaching . . . . . . . . 155

Epilogue . . . . . . . . . . . . . . . . . 175
References . . . . . . . . . . . . . . . . 177
Index . . . . . . . . . . . . . . . . . 183
Acknowledgments . . . . . . . . . . . . . . 193
About the Author . . . . . . . . . . . . . . 195

# Preface

This book is about applying Universal Design for Learning (UDL) in higher education contexts. It is intended primarily for those teaching in higher education, though it will be of use to anyone with an interest in learning, teaching, and assessment at any grade level—or in informal learning settings, for that matter—because the UDL Guidelines and principles apply wherever and whenever learning takes place.

An important part of becoming an expert learner, which is the purpose of UDL, involves achieving mastery over learning. The concept of mastering learning—that is, being able to apply a full range of practical and cognitive skills to learning content—is a central theme of the book. At its heart, this book is a hands-on guide on "how to teach." It provides clear-cut, practical advice on how to support learners to master their learning and become expert learners in line with UDL's key aim.

Since I am based in the United Kingdom, having spent my entire teaching career there, several of the perspectives, ideas, and examples presented are grounded in the UK higher education context. Despite the slightly UK-centric flavor, the ideas and examples presented are universally applicable.

In reality, reading this book alone probably won't be enough for you to master UDL. Reading it, reflecting on the advice it provides, and then adopting and modifying the guidance and suggestions to your own context may eventually help you to master UDL. Developing mastery will depend, as it always does, on practice, revision, and more practice. It is important to remember that nobody ever arrives at the point of perfection when it comes to teaching. Learning and teaching are constantly evolving, as learners and their expectations change, and particularly as technological changes alter the way in which we engage, interact with, and support learners. Therefore, effective teaching is an ongoing, iterative process that keeps evolving and adapting to ever-changing circumstances and contexts. The advice in this book will help you to become well prepared for maximizing that ongoing, iterative process.

The book is split into four parts. Part I introduces the purpose and place of UDL in higher education, stressing why UDL is so relevant and so important to modern higher education settings. Part II introduces the core, underlying principles related to gaining mastery over learning, placing specific emphasis on how teachers can optimize the time we spend with our learners to support them to become expert learners. Part II also introduces the *Cheese Sandwich* concept of supporting learning, which essentially provides the vehicle through which mastery over learning can happen. Part III explores the design aspects of supporting learners to become expert learners, placing specific focus on the core components of effective accessible, inclusive, and equitable learning design. Finally, Part IV is about how to put all of the advice in the book together to help you create learning experiences in which learners can be supported to achieve mastery over their learning and subsequently achieve the status of expert learner. This part also includes advice and guidance on how to effectively evaluate teaching practice as part of the ongoing iterative process of effective teaching.

Each chapter closes with a list of references and recommendations for further reading. Where possible, you should consult these resources to support your further learning of UDL, and effective learning and teaching practices more generally. Each chapter also contains various activities, tasks, and resources to get you reflectively thinking about your practice in terms of where it is now and how it can evolve as you continue to develop your skills. I recommend that you complete each activity as you go through the book.

Teaching can be a challenging endeavor. That's one of the reasons it is so rewarding. I'm not one for using crystal balls to predict the future, but I can confidently predict that you'll face struggles and make mistakes as you develop your UDL learning and teaching practices. You will find some learners difficult, and you will have days where nothing seems to go right. This is an inevitability, especially if you have been teaching according to a different, less learner-centered methodology, as most of us have at some point in our higher education career. Don't worry about mistakes or struggles. They are all part of the processes of adapting and improving.

I recognize that much of the information and advice in this book is idealized, making me sound like the perfect teacher, one who has always been able to seamlessly design and deliver effective learning experiences according to the UDL principles, with few challenges. Please understand that I am not the perfect teacher, I never have been, and I never will be—if indeed such things exist. I have faced many challenges and difficulties, and had many times where I wondered if teaching was the vocation for me. Let's be clear: It's totally fine to feel like that. Actually, it's natural to feel like that, especially if you are new to teaching. Please do not think that you will be able to apply every piece of advice and every suggestion in this book and get it perfect at all times in every situation. It is unlikely that you will ever be granted the optimal time and resources to create consistently perfect instructional experiences. Sometimes, you just have to do the best you can with the time and resources you have. As Winston Churchill once said, "Success is not final; failure is not fatal: It is the courage to continue that counts."

Enjoy the journey!

# Part I

# UDL and Modern Higher Education

# 1

# The Changing Nature of Higher Education

## Changes in Demographics, Policy, and How We See the World

Universal Design for Learning is an especially timely subject for a few reasons. First, the increased participation in higher education of students from varied backgrounds and circumstances—economic, racial, ethnic, and cultural as well as disability status—has changed the way we need to approach the design and delivery of learning experiences. Globally, from 2000 to 2022, participation in higher education has more than doubled from 100 million enrollments to more than 235 million, according to UNESCO (2022).

At the same time, the participation rates in higher education of students with identified disabilities have sharply increased across Western countries. For example, in the United Kingdom, the number of postsecondary learners declaring a disability increased 47 percent between 2015 and 2020 (Hubble & Bolton, 2020). Some of this change is driven by demographic shifts, and some is driven by policy. Countries like the United Kingdom, Canada, and the United States have strong legal guarantees to protect individuals from discrimination in higher education, including individuals with disabilities. Institutions in these countries have a legal duty to implement reasonable adjustments to ensure that learners with disabilities are not substantially disadvantaged when accessing education compared with nondisabled learners. Furthermore, governments are increasingly recognizing that physical access to the education spaces where learning takes place is only part of the challenge: Learners also need appropriate accommodations for learning, language, and intellectual differences.

Then there are the changes in work and career requirements. Growing skills gaps in the workforce mean that many working professionals are now required to engage, or reengage, with higher education as a means of developing new skills to meet demand. Furthermore, advances in technology and automation mean that many working professionals are required to rethink their careers as their jobs are transformed by technology or in some cases no longer required at all (World Economic Forum, 2020).

Given these changes, teachers can be fairly confident that the learners we teach will come from a range of backgrounds and will likely differ by gender, age, ethnicity, class, disability, sexual orientation, and faith, among other things. They will also arrive at university with a wide range of previous educational experiences and a diverse set of learning needs. They will have differing levels of motivation and learning confidence as well as diverse emotional needs. Such diversity means that the way in which modern learners learn will be subject to extreme variability. Thus, learning, and of course teaching, must account for this variability from the start as part of the way programs, courses, modules or units, and individual teaching sessions are designed and delivered. There is no such thing as a typical higher education learner today.

Then there are student expectations. Professor Jean Twenge of San Diego State University has written extensively about the *iGeneration* or *iGen*, the generation born between the mid-1990s and early 2010s (Twenge, 2017). iGen'ers, as Twenge refers to them, represent the first generation to grow up fully immersed in a world dominated by high-tech developments such as the internet, smartphones, and tablets (Twenge, 2017). iGen'ers are hardwired to the internet as a means of connecting with the world in their own personalized ways (Twenge, 2017). As a result, personalized and customizable experiences are not just a "nice to have" for iGen'ers but the expected norm.

Many learners from the iGeneration believe that learning experiences should represent a seamless extension of their personal experiences, in which mobile devices play a huge role. As with many aspects of modern life, iGen learners expect learning to be available on demand, an experience that can happen at any time and any place—much like television, music, and shopping—and reflects their individual needs and preferences, with few barriers preventing or reducing their engagement.

As well as wanting personalization and customization, some learners may *need* to customize their learning experience to reduce or remove barriers. During a fascinating discussion, renowned UDL expert Katie Novak used a lovely café analogy to explain to me the importance of offering choice and enabling customizability to support learning. If a customer of a café or coffee shop wanted a coffee with milk but was lactose intolerant, and the coffee shop did not serve alternative milks such as soy, oat, or coconut milk, then the customer would be excluded from enjoying coffee with milk. A simple example, perhaps, but it clearly illustrates that barriers are environmental and contextual. In this case, the shop's failure to provide alternative milks raises a barrier that makes the customer unable to enjoy their drink. The customer had a need and there was a clear barrier to that need being met: the absence of alternative milks. Such exclusions can happen in the same way when learners cannot meet their needs in learning situations due to environmental barriers.

This is where UDL comes in. At its heart, Universal Design for Learning (Meyer, Rose, & Gordon, 2014; Rose & Meyer, 2002) is a design framework that considers the variable ways in which different learners approach and engage with learning. Accordingly, a critical part of a UDL approach to learning, teaching, and assessment is to have a clear awareness of learner needs, preferences, and any barriers they may face to learning effectively.

## UDL AND HIGHER EDUCATION

This book has been influenced by and will hopefully build upon the growing literature on the application of UDL in higher education settings. In recent years, important contributions and resources in this area have helped support our understanding of UDL in college or university settings. Some of these works have focused on the strategies, tactics, and resources required for gaining institutional "buy-in" for UDL, as well as its strategic adoption and implementation (Black & Moore, 2019; Fovet, 2020; Fovet, 2021).

Similar work has sought to demonstrate best practices in UDL implementation in international settings, drawing on worldwide research to provide strategies for enhancing accessibility, engagement, and learning outcomes through flexible approaches to learning and teaching (Bracken & Novak, 2019). Other works have raised awareness of the universality of UDL, showing clearly how UDL benefits all learners, not just learners with disabilities (Tobin & Behling, 2018), and providing practical guidance for educators to apply UDL to their learning and teaching approaches. Other publications have focused on the perception of UDL among college and university staff and students in a variety of settings (Black, Weinberg, & Brodwin, 2015; Kennette & Wilson, 2019; Merry, 2023), with several works demonstrating the effectiveness of UDL in higher education settings (Davies, Schelly, & Spooner, 2013; Schelly, Davies, & Spooner, 2011; Smith, 2012). Furthermore, some excellent web-based resources, such as CAST's UDL on Campus website (*http://udloncampus.cast.org/home*), have further advanced our understanding of how to apply UDL in higher education settings in terms of curriculum design, media, materials, and policy. This book assimilates all the knowledge and understanding from those resources, as well as that gained from many more sources, but with a focus on instructional design and delivery. This is a "how to teach" book that dissects the major parts of the instructional experience and reinterprets them through a UDL lens.

One note about terms: Throughout this book, you will encounter the terms *program*, *course*, *module*, and *unit*. For the purposes of this book, the latter three are used interchangeably. Each represents a unit of teaching that covers an individual subject for which learners experience a fixed schedule of classes or sessions typically lasting a term or semester. Learners must successfully complete an entire collection of courses, modules, or units to achieve an academic degree, which in this book is known as a *program*.

**PAUSE AND THINK** Without thinking too long or too hard about it, can you identify any potential barriers in the learning environments you create for your learners? Is there anything that forms part of the learning environment that could exclude any of your learners or prevent them from learning in the most effective way?

# 2
# Universal Design for Learning

As described previously, the UDL (Rose & Meyer, 2002) design framework considers the variable ways in which different learners approach and engage with learning. A UDL approach to learning, teaching, and assessment requires a clear awareness of learner needs, preferences, and any barriers they may face to learning effectively.

The ultimate purpose of UDL is to support learners to become *expert learners* (Meyer et al., 2014). An expert learner can be defined as one who not only is able to master learning content by applying a full range of cognitive and practical skills to it, but also is aware of their own personal approach to achieving that mastery (as summarized in Figure 2-1). It is important to keep in mind that the UDL approach calls for separating the goals of learning from the means of achieving them. Therefore, if the goal of learning is to achieve mastery over content, then different learners will have a different means of achieving that mastery, which is why a UDL approach to instructional design embraces personalization and customization, as discussed in Chapter 1. (Note that this book uses the terms *goals* and *learning goals* interchangeably with the terms *outcomes* and *learning outcomes*. These terms all represent the same concept—the things learners must "know" or be able to "do" as a result of their learning.)

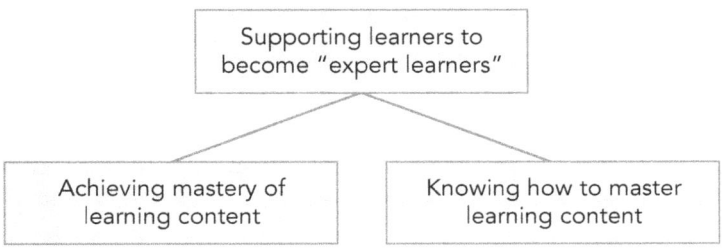

**FIGURE 2-1.** Two prongs of expert learning

A second important characteristic of UDL and its aim of supporting learners to become expert learners is the role of metacognition as an inherent part of the learning process and experience. Becoming aware of one's own personal approach to achieving mastery over learning content is effectively about learning to learn, a critical skill in becoming an expert learner as well as a required skill for lifelong learning. Hence, UDL supports learners to learn effectively not only in the here and now on the units and programs they take as part of their higher education experience, but also in their endeavors beyond higher education.

Although UDL originates in neuroscience, because this is a "how to teach" book I'll keep the neuroscience light. Becoming an expert learner is related to three connected, interdependent neural networks in the brain: the *strategic, recognition,* and *affective* networks (Rose & Meyer, 2002). Thinking about the three broad networks can be helpful when designing instructional experiences. UDL recognizes that no two brains will be identical with respect to the three networks, and intentionally targets the variability within each network.

Specifically, the UDL framework recognizes variability in *engagement,* or the "why" of learning (affective network), which is related to learner interest, motivation, persistence, and self-regulation. Note that *engagement* here doesn't represent some sort of fun or participation barometer as it's sometimes defined in higher education; rather, engagement from a UDL perspective is essentially about the level of attention and commitment demonstrated by learners in learning scenarios.

> **PAUSE AND THINK** Think about your current teaching approaches:
> - How do you currently recruit interest in your learners? What alternative ways could you recruit interest?
> - How do you currently make sure your learners sustain effort and persist with their learning? What else could you do to make sure your learners sustain effort and persistence?
> - How do you currently ensure that your learners can self-regulate their learning? What else could you do to support self-regulation in your learners?

The instructional approaches that produce optimal levels of attention and commitment will vary for different learners. For example, some learners may enjoy working on individual tasks, whereas others may prefer working in groups with peers. Some learners may enjoy unstructured tasks allowing freedom, whereas others may prefer tasks with clear structure and guidelines. Some learners may achieve a state of optimal attention and commitment in didactic learning scenarios, such as a lecture where their role is principally to be a passive recipient of information transmission. Conversely, for other learners, a lecture may negatively impact their level of attention and commitment, thereby posing a barrier to learning. Such learners may achieve an optimal state of attention and commitment in more active learning scenarios—for example, collaborating with peers to solve problems. The point is that optimizing attention and commitment, and thus engagement, among a community of learners will require a variety of approaches; one-size-fits-all is unlikely to optimize engagement for all learners and will erect barriers for some. Hence, educators should provide options, and not simply for the sake of doing so, but to remove or reduce barriers. For example, if a group task presents a barrier to a particular learner learning effectively, can you offer them an individual task option to help remove that barrier?

The UDL framework also recognizes variability in *representation*, or the "what" of learning (recognition network), which relates to perceptions of language, symbols, and comprehension. Representation perhaps exerts its greatest influence on the learning resources and materials we produce and share with our learners. For example, learners will differ in how they perceive and comprehend information related to learning; some may be happy with text-based learning resources requiring them to read, whereas others may prefer having the same information presented via multimedia options such as a video or podcast. Traditionally in higher education, learning resources have largely consisted of text-based materials that often must be printed and read. For a learner who finds reading and comprehending large amounts of text a challenge—such as one with dyslexia or one for whom English is a second language—providing only text-based learning resources that cannot be modified represents a barrier to learning. In such a scenario, it's important to think about alternative resources that could reduce or remove the barriers posed by reading large amounts of text. Also consider how you might provide the resources in modifiable formats so that learners can alter font sizes, styles, colors, and the like. Again, learners should be given options and choices in relation to learning resources to reduce or remove barriers. Can those learners who struggle to read text presented in, say, journal articles or books be offered the same information in a different format, such as a video, a podcast, or even a written summary, to reduce barriers?

> **PAUSE AND THINK** Think about your current learning resources and materials:
>
> - What considerations do you currently make when designing and creating learning resources? Do you need to consider anything else?
> - How do you currently ensure a multisensory learning experience? What else could you do to support multisensory learning?
> - What do you currently do to support learner mastery of subject-specific vocabulary? What else could you do?
> - What do you currently do to provide options that support varied ways of receiving and processing (summarizing, categorizing, prioritizing, contextualizing) information? What else could you do?
> - What do you currently do to activate and build background knowledge among your learners? What else could you do?
> - How do you currently use learning resources to help learners make sense of content? How else could you use them?

Finally, the framework recognizes variability in *action and expression*, or the "how" (strategic network) of learning, which relates to expression, communication, physical action, and executive function. Action and expression relates most closely to the ways in which learners demonstrate their learning, and thus has important implications for how we formally assess learning (summative assessment), as well as how we informally assess and evaluate learning in instructional scenarios, which may include formative assessment and simply checking understanding.

Learners will differ in the ways in which they are able to demonstrate their understanding. For example, some learners may be able to express themselves in writing well, whereas others may be better able to demonstrate their understanding verbally.

Frequently, assessments are designed in such a way that they erect barriers. For example, consider a biology exam that has the primary purpose of assessing biology knowledge. Let's say the exam is handwritten, undertaken without prior knowledge of the questions, without learner access to learning resources, and under strictly timed conditions. In addition to assessing biology knowledge, the exam also unintentionally assesses several irrelevant factors, such as handwriting, spelling, time management, and memory, to name but a few. Subsequently, the exam erects barriers that prevent some learners from clearly demonstrating their biology knowledge. To reduce barriers in this scenario, you could allow learners to word-process the exam, and make the exam both *seen* and *open book*, allowing learners to see the questions in advance and use resources to help them during the exam. Removing time restrictions would also reduce a barrier. An alternative approach is to use a completely different assessment method; is an exam the only way a learner can demonstrate biology knowledge? Is it the most authentic way? Again, the point here is that learners should be provided with options and choices about how they demonstrate their learning in order to reduce or remove barriers. For example, some learners may struggle with the English language and have challenges communicating in written form, which presents a learning barrier. Could they be offered an alternative means of expressing themselves, such as through a presentation or verbal discussion, to remove the barrier posed by writing?

**PAUSE AND THINK** Think about how your learners currently demonstrate learning:

- How do you know learners have achieved the learning goals for individual teaching sessions?
- When checking learner understanding, do you require all learners to demonstrate learning in the same way? If yes, could some learners be disadvantaged by this?
- When giving learners an assessment task (summative or formative), do you provide examples of different plans and strategies they could use to support completion of the task?

Engagement, representation, and action and expression represent the three principles of UDL, and Figure 2-2 illustrates the need to provide options and choices in relation to each. According to the UDL Guidelines (CAST, 2018; Meyer et al., 2014), becoming an expert learner requires a learner to become "purposeful and motivated," which is the ultimate goal of the engagement principle; "resourceful and knowledgeable," which is the ultimate goal of the representation principle; and "strategic and goal-directed," which is the ultimate goal of the action and expression principle. The UDL framework recognizes that learners will have different needs, preferences, and barriers in relation to the three UDL principles.

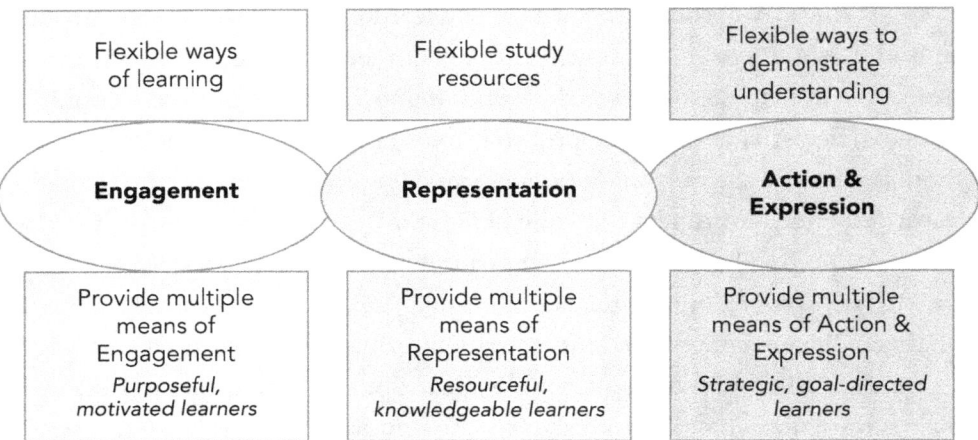

**FIGURE 2-2.** The UDL principles. © 2018 CAST, Inc. Adapted with permission.

These are the reasons why the UDL framework espouses multiple means of engagement, representation, and action and expression. UDL allows learners to personalize critical aspects of their learning experience to support their preferences or minimize barriers they face. In this regard, the UDL approach of providing multiple options not only reduces or removes barriers but also closely aligns with the desire for personalization and customizability that many learners in modern higher education may expect (as explored in Chapter 1). Indeed, UDL is perhaps a better fit for today's learners than more traditional approaches to learning and teaching in higher education, where everyone is largely expected to engage with and approach learning in the same way. For example, content has traditionally been delivered as lectures, learning resources have consisted exclusively of text-based materials requiring lots of reading, and assessments have overly relied on written conceptions of understanding, requiring strong written communication skills. If you experienced this model and struggled with it, then you were the party considered to be at fault, not the model. The barrier was in you, not in the environment.

UDL is about reversing this idea. Barriers exist in the environment, not in the learner, and UDL is focused on removing them to help students develop as expert learners.

Accordingly, instructional strategies and approaches should be designed and delivered to fit the learners, not the other way around. In the past, the expert learner was someone motivated to learn by sitting and listening to an academic pontificate, sometimes for hours, about a particular topic. They likely preferred and were skilled at learning through listening and through reading and comprehending large amounts of text, and could demonstrate their learning in writing, usually under oppressively timed conditions. This may have worked well when universities were able to hand-pick the strongest learners and when learning communities were a largely homogenous group in terms of demographic makeup and learning needs and preferences. However, today—when universities have never been more diverse across all categories—the traditional approach will not work for everyone.

## ADOPTING A UDL MINDSET

Unfortunately, many teachers in higher education still believe that successful learning stems from innate learner characteristics, such as intelligence, IQ, aptitude, and talent. Even more unfortunate is the fact that many learners agree with them, feeling that their capability for learning is fixed and cannot be changed. Perhaps the starting point in developing a UDL mindset is to lose this belief if it is one you currently hold. As Professor John Hattie's work has so importantly found, teachers have the largest impact on learner achievement (Hattie, 2012). Therefore, begin your UDL journey by believing that teachers can make a difference.

The next important step is to reflect. Every teacher has an idea or mindset about learning and teaching—a set of assumptions, views, beliefs, and even biases about how effective learning happens. This mindset will influence the approaches and strategies you use to support effective learning, as well as the approaches and strategies that you *don't* use. Your mindset subconsciously guides everything you do from a learning and teaching perspective, from the way you design and plan instructional experiences to the way in which you assess and give feedback. However, your mindset about learning and teaching must be challenged if you are to fully embrace UDL and apply it effectively; none of the tools and teaching strategies in the world will make a difference to your learners if you don't challenge your own beliefs about what an effective learning experience is. One of the biggest potential barriers we face to adopting UDL effectively is the belief that "our way" of supporting effective learning is "the way" it should be done. There are many different approaches and pathways that can support effective learning, and we must embrace them.

The most effective teachers are those who are constantly modifying their practice—those who are regularly requesting feedback from their learners and peers, intentionally reflecting on their practice, and subsequently learning how to teach more effectively using evidence-based approaches. Becoming an effective UDL practitioner requires precisely this approach. Effective UDL practice is an iterative process, an ongoing journey that requires a continual dialogue with learners about how they can be most effectively supported. Intentional improvement is a core value of the effective UDL practitioner, as we will explore more closely in Chapter 15.

## EXAMINING VALUES

Another important step on the journey to becoming an effective UDL practitioner is to examine your values as a teacher. UDL is essentially a value-driven approach to learning, teaching, and assessment. Values are those factors that we consider crucial in relation to how we want to live and go about our daily activities. We use values to regulate the priorities in our lives and to measure the level of success we attain. UDL practitioners embrace inclusion, accessibility, and equitability as values key to the learning experience. They believe that education is about transforming lives by acting as a catalyst for social justice—promoting inclusion, fairness, access, and equity for all learners, irrespective of their background or starting point. How do your own values align? Generally speaking, UDL practitioners value:

- All learners, their uniqueness, their personal experience, their ongoing progress and development, and their ambitions for learning and for life

- The cognitive, social, emotional, and collective potential of learning for all

- Equality, diversity, and inclusion in all aspects of learning and life

- Intentional and lifelong improvement of teaching and/or support of learning

- Collaboration with others for the benefit of enhancing learning for all

- A learning environment conducive to physical and emotional safety

- A learning environment that is inclusive, accessible, and equitable, and supports learner interest, attention, effort, and commitment

- Regular communication with learners about their needs, preferences, and barriers they face to learning effectively

- The use of a wide range of learning resources, including technology, to break down barriers and support the needs of all learners

At the core, UDL practitioners believe in equity. This does not mean treating all learners the same, it means adapting to each learner's diverse and unique needs. Therefore, we must make a special and deliberate effort to learn about and meet the needs of individual learners by reducing or removing barriers to their learning. UDL is an enabler and equalizer that allows all learners to participate effectively in learning irrespective of the barriers they may face. As discussed in Chapter 1, we can fully expect and anticipate that modern learners in higher education won't be a homogenous group. They will likely be an exceptionally diverse group, with each learner bringing a unique set of experiences and needs to the learning environment.

## ADDRESSING THE TIME CONUNDRUM

Making a commitment to removing barriers through inclusive, accessible, equitable learning may seem daunting. Many teachers I've worked with over the years have told me they simply don't have the time to implement UDL. Regardless of the type of institution you work in, you're likely stretched for time, and there's no denying that designing inclusive, accessible, and equitable learning in line with UDL takes time. UDL is not a "quick and dirty" endeavor. In most cases, it represents a comprehensive undoing of all we have ever known about learning and teaching. Effective learning design takes time, and it's not possible to quickly throw a plan together and expect it to support all learners to effectively achieve learning goals. We have to think carefully, get feedback, think again, modify, and repeat this cycle, working iteratively to support dynamic needs among our learners. However, we should remember that anything worth achieving takes time. Success is a journey, usually an extended one, and the road may well be strewn with temporary setbacks as you learn how to apply UDL effectively in your own context. Make sure you have realistic expectations. You will not become an expert practitioner of UDL overnight, and you may only be able to make small, gradual changes to your practice. As the saying goes, "slow and steady wins the race," and it's useful to keep this in mind as you develop your UDL learning and teaching practices. The time you invest in UDL is justified by the potential payoff for learners. There's little point in being highly efficient in how you develop your practice and subsequently design learning experiences if the learners are not learning anything. In this sense, efficiency is contingent upon effectiveness. Finally, revisit your values when thinking about the time investment required to develop your UDL practice. If you truly value inclusive, accessible, and equitable learning that removes barriers and gives everyone a chance to reach their potential not only as a learner but also as a human being, then you must find the time. Institutions of education exist for one purpose: to support learners to learn effectively. Thus, everything we do, no matter how long it takes, should be directed at this aim.

You must become adept at using the limited time you have as efficiently and effectively as possible. Through continual evaluation, you can regularly update your learning resources, session plans, and learning activities, which will save time in the long run. Create a bank of resources, artifacts, plans, and activities that you can routinely draw from to help you save time.

> **PAUSE AND THINK** Without thinking too long or too hard about it, can you identify the factors that shape your attitudes and values as a teacher? What characteristics do you associate with yourself from a teaching perspective? Subject expertise? Kindness? Warmth? A commitment to equality? Sense of humor?

# 3

# Learner Variability

As we've explored, learners in higher education come from a range of backgrounds, likely differing by gender, age, ethnicity, class, disability, sexual orientation, and faith. They also arrive in higher education with broad and diverse educational experiences, learning preferences, and cultural capital, as well as differing levels of motivation and learning confidence. They will also possess a diverse set of emotional needs. Each learner is unique, possessing individual needs that must be fulfilled if they are to learn effectively. We can't simply try to guess the needs of the "average learner" in our teaching sessions. When we teach from a UDL perspective, there's no such thing as an average learner (Meyer et al., 2014; Rose & Meyer, 2002). It is critical that we learn about and meet individual learner needs, specifically addressing barriers they may face to learning effectively. Our ability to do so is often the critical factor that determines their level of learning success.

Since modern higher education is exceptionally diverse, we can expect a high level of learner variability among the learners that we teach. *Learner variability* can be defined as everything that may influence a learner's engagement with and approach to their learning and will ultimately have an impact upon their ability to successfully gain mastery over their learning. It is essentially all the ways in which learners differ from one another (Meyer et al., 2014).

Some sources of learner variability are obvious. For example, an international learner whose first language is not English would engage with and approach learning very differently from a "home" learner fluent in English. A learner with dyslexia, who may have difficulties processing and remembering information that they hear and see, will engage with and approach learning in a very different way than a learner who is not dyslexic. However, some sources of variability are less obvious. For example, culture can have an important influence on how we learn. A research study by Jonathan B. Freeman and his collaborators presents an interesting example. In the study, American and Japanese participants were shown a series of drawings of characters in dominant or subordinate postures. The drawings showing dominant body postures appeared to trigger neural responses in the reward domain in American people, but the opposite was true for Japanese people: They instead demonstrated responses in the reward domain when shown the drawings of characters in subordinate postures (Freeman, Rule, Adams, & Ambady, 2009). The different value systems of American and Japanese societies, and the different learned behaviors within the two cultures, were cited as the main reasons for divergent responses between American and Japanese participants (Freeman et al., 2009).

Different cultures see and understand the world differently. Therefore, culture is a potential source of learner variability. Different cultures can learn different things, as in the preceding example, or they can learn about the same ideas and concepts but in a different way. As a result, we must be aware of how the information we pass on to our learners is interpreted and subsequently understood. Culture clearly influences the way in which people interpret information and subsequently respond to various stimuli (Chita-Tegmark, Gravel, Maria De Lourdes, Domings, & Rose, 2012; Freeman et al., 2009).

It is also important to remember that some sources of variability will not be fixed, and as such will not be entirely predictable. For example, not only are we different from each other, but our individual needs are always changing. Human beings are dynamic in this way. We cannot know exactly what a learner might need in tomorrow's session, because we don't know what mood that learner might be in, how much sleep they got last night, how bored or motivated they will be, or if they had an argument with a parent or partner before coming to class, for example. In this regard, learners are a "moving target" with constantly changing needs. Indeed, factors such as lack of sleep, lack of motivation, boredom, and the like are regarded as *reverse effects*—elements that have an entirely negative impact upon successful learning and attainment—by Professor John Hattie in his immense book *Visible Learning for Teachers* (Hattie, 2012). Therefore, it is critically important that we make the goals of learning firm and clear, explicitly detailing what the learners are required to know or do as a result of their learning. Our role is then to support learners to achieve those goals by enabling them to make choices about their learning based on where they are at that specific point in time. In other words, what do they need to be successful with their learning right at that specific moment?

Our inability to predict all sources of learner variability is one of the central reasons why effective UDL practice is iterative. It is a process that requires—indeed, relies on—continual learner feedback. We must constantly evaluate, review, and modify our teaching based on feedback from learners. If we don't make a continual effort to check in with our learners, we probably won't ever meet their needs optimally. Offering choices based on feedback is central to the process of supporting learners in gaining a sharper awareness of what helps them to learn most effectively, which itself is part of the pathway to becoming an expert learner, as discussed in Chapter 2.

> **PAUSE AND THINK** Think about a group of learners that you teach. What makes those learners different from each other? Will those differences influence the way in which they approach and engage with learning?

Many texts on learning and teaching will broadly state that there are three components that support good teaching and effective learning: 1) the teaching or instruction; 2) the curriculum; and 3) the assessment. Critically, the teacher is responsible for ensuring that each component operates optimally so that each learner experiences instruction that enables them to master the curriculum, as demonstrated in them performing well in their assessments. Unfortunately, most teaching in higher education over the years has completely discounted the unique needs of learners from this model. Instead, teaching has often been about the transmission of the curriculum from teacher to learner over a given time period, with the focus on content coverage, and very little room for considering learner variability. We might say that this is a *teacher-centered* approach to learning and teaching. However, to support effective learning in our learners, we must make the shift to a *learner-centered* approach. Understanding and planning for learner variability is the critical starting point for adopting a learner-centered approach, because understanding the variability of your learners means understanding the types of barriers they may face when learning. Most importantly, with this approach you'll begin to understand how you can remove those barriers and support effective learning in all of your learners, not just a fortunate few.

**PAUSE AND THINK: DINNER-PARTY EXERCISE** The following thought exercise, introduced to me by Katie Novak, serves to illustrate the importance and place of learner variability. It's very simple but will help you understand that a one-size-fits-all approach to anything will not work.

- Imagine you are planning a dinner party for a group of people that you have never met.
- What variability would you expect in relation to the dietary needs and preferences of your guests?
- How would you plan for the variability in their dietary needs and preferences?

## GETTING TO KNOW YOUR LEARNERS

The starting point to planning for learner variability is to get to know your learners. Perhaps one of the greatest commodities we can have as teachers is information. Therefore, it is important to derive as much information about your learners as you can. Demographic information can be useful—for example, age, gender, race, ethnicity, disability status (including learning differences), language preference, entry qualifications or scores, or grades achieved in other or related modules or units.

In addition to demographic data, it can also be really useful to include some sort of diagnostic assessment of prior learning during your instructional planning. Remember, some learners will already have experience and knowledge of the topic you'll be teaching, whereas others will have none. Thus, each learner's approach to and engagement with the topic could be very different. This is why it's worthwhile to find out a little about what they already know and how they feel about the topic you're going to teach. For example, some learners may be very excited about the prospect of tackling algebraic equations, whereas others may be absolutely terrified! Either way, their feelings about the topic, which will likely have been determined by their previous experiences with it, will impact their engagement and approach to it.

Demographic data and diagnostic assessment, although worthwhile, will be useful only up to a point. Perhaps of greater importance is data on the way in which the learners approach and engage with their learning, since this type of information will give you a clearer idea of how they learn most effectively. Because the sources of learner variability are very broad and too numerous to mention here, I've always found it useful to group them into four categories:

- Learning attitudes and mindset
- Interest and learning needs
- Social and emotional learning
- Cultural relevance and perspectives

Sometimes it can be useful to plan teaching sessions by observing these four categories from a variability and barriers perspective. For example, how might your learners vary in each category, and what barriers does your learning environment pose as a result? If your learning environment is filled with resources that are very American- or Euro-centric, will this pose a barrier for the non-American and European learners in your group? I remember having a learner in my class once who was autistic. The learner did not engage in the group activities that I set because they said that one of the traits of their autism was that they preferred to work independently. Hence, the group activities that I had designed into my session were a barrier. What can you do as the teacher to remove such barriers as part of your planning? Let's take a closer look at each category in turn.

## Learning Attitudes and Mindset

The category of learning attitudes and mindset relates to learner self-perception, their interest in learning, their perceived role in the learning environment, their motivation for learning, and ultimately their engagement in the learning. It relates to the way learners feel about themselves—specifically, their confidence, competence, and role in the learning situation.

To find out more about your learners' learning attitudes and mindset, you could survey them to gauge their interest in and attitude toward learning, or you could, as part of an introductory session, get them to explore their perceived role in their learning (for example, are they there to be a passive or active participant in the learning?). You could find out about learner motivations for study; this is what Phil Race calls the "want" and the "need" for learning. Why do they want to learn? Why do they need to learn? Race says effective learning cannot happen without adequate motivation, so it's vitally important that you have some idea of what motivates your learners (Race, 2019). It's always useful for learners to explore both their perceived learning strengths and weaknesses. These can be generic or specific to the subject you teach. Finally, it can be useful to explore whether the learners have any personal learning ambitions or targets. If they don't, it can be equally useful to help them to set some, especially from the motivational point of view. Personal learning targets can be linked to the learning outcomes or goals for your teaching session, modules, or units—or even entire programs.

## Interest and Learning Needs

The category of interest and learning needs refers to the level of curiosity that the learner brings to the learning situation. It represents their needs in terms of task type and resource type, and their capability for self-direction—which is very important in higher education, since, traditionally, approximately two-thirds of learning is self-directed. Interest and learning needs also reflect how learners like to demonstrate their understanding in learning situations. Hence, the application of the UDL principles of engagement, representation, and action and expression is especially important when you're thinking about and planning for learner interest and learning needs.

To learn more about your learners' interest and learning needs, you could survey them or ask them about content or topics that interest them or make them curious; this supports co-creation of the curriculum, which may also support engagement. It can be useful to find out about the types of learning tasks and activities that learners prefer or feel support their learning most effectively. For example, do they prefer problem solving, independent tasks, collaborative work, or creative tasks? In many scenarios, your teaching will represent the learners' first experiences of a topic. Therefore, in addition to assessing their prior understanding, you might also find it useful to ask how they like to learn about new topics—for example, do they prefer to learn in an immersive fashion, or do they prefer to have the key information summarized first? Do they like to discover new topics for themselves or solve problems related to the topic?

Since higher education is very heavily influenced by self-directed study, learners must be provided with resources for independent learning. Therefore, it can be a good strategy to find out about their resource needs. For example, do they prefer written or text-based documents, video, audio, images, and websites, or a balance of different types of resources? It's also very important that you understand how your learners feel about self-directed learning, and their perceived level of competence with it. When it comes to formative and summative assessment, it can be useful to find out about their needs, as well as any dislikes they may have and why. Critically, if the assessments for the modules or units you teach cannot be changed, you must find out how learners feel about the assessment methods so that you can provide stronger support, especially in circumstances where the learners dislike the method being used, such as an exam. Rather than change the assessment, you can support their approach to exams and hopefully improve their exam skills through practice.

## Social and Emotional Learning

Learning is a social activity as well as an emotional one. The science is complicated and beyond the scope of this book, but we can at least be clear that emotion significantly influences cognition (Immordino-Yang & Damasio, 2007), impacting perception, attention, memory, reasoning, and problem solving—all important processes inherent in learning (Tyng, Amin, Saad, & Malik, 2017). Furthermore, cognition is influenced by social factors. For example, we quickly identify the presence of other learners in our learning environment. Consequently, we align our attention with theirs, influencing how we perceive our environment, as well as how we represent and remember things (Kampis & Southgate, 2020). For these reasons, it's important to consider the social and emotional learning needs of your learners. This includes their responses to individual learning as well as to group learning. We all know the challenges of getting learners to work in groups, particularly on assessed work, so you should understand how your learners feel about it.

Social learning also relates to the learner's perceived value to their learning group, the perceived value of social behaviors associated with learning, and how the learner responds to differentiation. For example, have you ever been placed in a tiered group or set in a learning situation? If you were in the "top" group, it likely made you feel good about your competence in whatever subject you were learning about. Conversely, if you were not in the top group, or if you were in the "bottom" one, how did that make you feel? I remember being placed in the bottom group for geography at school and feeling it was hugely unfair, because I believed my geography knowledge warranted my being put in a higher group. I grew to dislike geography and the teacher who placed me in the bottom group, and subsequently I didn't engage with geography to the extent that I perhaps could have—all because of differentiation! Had the teacher explained to me that I was being placed in the bottom group so that I could receive more support with my learning and that I might move up to a higher group if I did well, then I may have felt differently. Hence, it's very important to differentiate appropriately and to explain the reasons for your approach to differentiation as well as make it clear that grouping is flexible. Remember, as a teacher, you play a huge role in how your learners feel when they are learning, and this can influence their well-being and subsequent success with their learning. There is more information on differentation and differentiated instruction in Chapter 5.

It's also very important to recognize that the learning environments we create will naturally elicit emotional responses from our learners. Regardless of whether those responses are positive or negative, we must recognize that, as teachers, we have a major responsibility to determine how our learners are feeling when they learn. This is very important for UDL, because at its core UDL is about reducing or removing barriers within the learning environment. Creating a learning environment that consistently elicits negative emotional responses and feelings is essentially adding barriers to the learning environment. For example, imagine a learner called upon during a seminar to solve a complex equation on the whiteboard in front of a whole class of peers. The learner may perceive the task as threatening since failing to solve the equation correctly may result in humiliation in front of their peers. Subsequently, the learner develops an emotional response characterized by a high level of anxiety. The unpleasant feelings of anxiety associated with being humiliated in front of their peers could negatively impact their ability to learn the equation effectively. In this scenario, the barrier isn't that the learner's emotional response to threat gives rise to feelings of anxiety, it's in the fact that the learner struggles to learn the equation effectively because they've been placed into a threatening situation that the teacher intentionally designed into the learning environment.

To learn more about the social and emotional learning aspects of your learners, you will find it useful to gauge their views on both independent and group working. Both learning types will likely feature heavily as part of the curriculum you deliver, so an aversion to either type could adversely affect learner motivation, engagement, and commitment. People don't tend to learn or demonstrate their learning very well when they're anxious, so try to find out about situations that may evoke an anxious response from your learners. When learners say they don't like exams, to what extent is their dislike for exams due to the anxiety they feel about taking them? I'd say it's usually a large part of it!

From a social perspective, all learners have a role to play because they will naturally form part of a learning community within the classroom. Accordingly, learners are highly valuable to each other as an important source of peer support. They are also a huge asset to the teacher because, in large classes particularly, peer learning and support can be important strategies to support learning among all learners. Therefore, it is important to gauge how learners perceive their value to others.

When it comes to the balance between independent learning and group learning, ask the learners what they feel they do well individually, and what they feel they do well in groups. It can also be helpful to find out which task types learners like to do independently. In some circumstances this information can be used to form groups for group work, as well as to provide task differentiation and task options—for example, some learners can be assigned an individual task while some can work in groups, or everyone can at least have the option.

Try to find out a little bit about your learners' peer working preferences. For example, are they comfortable working with other learners who have a superior level of knowledge or experience, or do they want to work only with learners at the same level? Are they happy to work in pairs but not in groups or vice versa? Finally, it can be a good idea to find out about your learners' attitudes toward supporting and helping others, particularly if you intend to include peer learning and support in your sessions. For learners who prefer to work independently, group work can be frustrating and therefore diminish their motivation for learning.

## Cultural Relevance and Perspectives

Cultural relevance is about the cultural learning perspectives that your learners bring to the learning environment and acknowledging the influence of culture on how learners perceive, interpret, and subsequently respond to various information and stimuli. As demonstrated earlier in this chapter with the example of American and Japanese responses to dominant and subordinate postures, culture influences how people learn (Freeman et al., 2009). Therefore, it is critical that all learners are represented in the curriculum—that they can see themselves in what they are being taught—so that the curriculum is culturally relevant to them. It is also useful to think about the cultural norms that influence your learning environment. Does your learning environment currently reflect your own dominant cultural norms? Does it reflect the typical or standard social norms of your cultural group, and, if so, is this appropriate given the cultural profile of the group you are about to teach?

To learn more about the cultural relevance and perspective aspects of your learners, it's very important to find out how your learners, especially those from nondominant racial and cultural backgrounds, perceive the learning experience. Subsequently, it can be useful to get your learners to reflect on how their cultural background influences their learning so that you can identify any blocks or barriers in your learning environment. Check out the "Exploring Identity and Cultural Norms" activity later in the chapter for guidance on how to do this.

The learning environment tends to reflect the cultural norms and values of the dominant cultural group within the classroom. Thus, in addition to having learners reflect, teachers should also consider the dominant cultural norms or values represented in the classroom: Do these need to be modified to better represent the learners? Are there any possible barriers? Frequently, the learning environments we create as teachers reflect our own cultural norms; that is, the values, ethos, content, language, symbols, learning resources, and general presentation of ideas and information may be rooted in our own personal, cultural view of the world, which could be at odds with the cultural identities of our learners or with the geographic area within which the learning is taking place. For example, Leicester, where I work, is one of the most culturally diverse cities in the UK, with 55 percent of the population composed of nonwhite inhabitants, approximately 70 different languages spoken, and at least 14 different faiths practiced. Contemplating whether the learning environment reflects the wider cultural makeup of the local geographic area can ensure it is authentic and representative of the world outside the classroom. Again, the "Exploring Identity and Cultural Norms" activity later in the chapter can help you here.

Reflecting on the cultural norms and values emphasized in your learning environment is the starting point for creating a more culturally sensitive learning environment. As you know, UDL is ultimately about removing or reducing barriers to ensure that learners are not excluded from learning. Making the learning experience more reflective of the learners removes a potential barrier and precursor to exclusion. Being aware of such barriers and then working to remove them may support a sense of belonging, engagement, and subsequent achievement among the learners, which is the essence of what we're trying to achieve.

Another important and related point is to remain in consistent dialogue with your learners by gaining regular feedback on their learning experiences. Just because the learning environment reflects the cultural norms and values of a dominant group in week one, for example, doesn't mean that it cannot change as the rest of the term or semester plays out. You can continually adapt and shape the curriculum and subsequent learning environment to reflect the learners' cultural and racial diversity, which is best done through co-creation with the learners. This will help you to answer the reflective question as to how differences in race and culture are represented in your curriculum. Use the learners to help you develop the content and give them the responsibility to make decisions. Being responsible for something, especially something important, tends to get people engaged. It is their learning environment, after all. Finally, based on the demographic information you have, which gives you an idea of the level of cultural diversity in your learning group, what other information on cultural perspectives about learning can you glean about your learning group?

Understanding the cultural relevance and perspectives of your learners will better enable you to support their learning through the options you provide them with in the classroom. For example, allowing them to choose topics or means of assessment reflective of their cultural identity and providing them with culturally representative examples, role models, and mentors will go a long way toward supporting their sense of belonging and engagement. There is transformative power in getting to know your learners!

## GATHERING INFORMATION ON YOUR LEARNERS

Gathering information on your learners may seem like a daunting and time-consuming prospect. For this reason, as a starting point, it can be useful to use a predetermined tool, such as a questionnaire or survey on learning preference or learning approach. Some common examples include the Inventory of Learning Styles in Higher Education (Vermunt, 1998), the Approaches and Study Skills Inventory for Learners (Tait, Entwistle, & McCune, 1998), the Learning and Study Strategies Inventory (Weinstein, Palmer, & Schulte, 1987), and the Motivated Strategies for Learning Questionnaire (Zeegers, 2001).

### EXPLORING IDENTITY AND CULTURAL NORMS ACTIVITY

As a teacher, exploring your own identity and better understanding the cultural norms espoused in your classroom is essential to becoming more culturally competent and ultimately supports greater racial and cultural equity. A good way to do this is to engage in a reflective activity based on answering the following questions:

- How would you define your cultural background? Why do you define it in the way you do? Has it always been this way or has it changed over time? Will it change in the future?

> - How does your cultural background influence your teaching? Does it influence how you engage with learners?
> - How does your cultural background influence the way you learn? How does it influence how you approach studying?
> - What impact does your cultural background have on your subject discipline? Can you identify your cultural background clearly within your discipline?
>
> It can be fun to answer these questions in a playful and creative way, using drawings, pictures, LEGO bricks, or modeling clay, for example.
>
> This activity can also be done with learners as part of an induction session or tutorial.
>
> Capturing the information that the learners provide on their cultural identity is an essential step in planning your curriculum and instruction, since both should reflect the learners they've been created for.
>
> This is a great way for learners and teachers to get to know each other and begin developing a compassionate, culturally competent learning community.

The VARK (Fleming & Mills, 1992) questionnaire—which stands for visual, aural, read-write, and kinesthetic—has been a popular choice within education for many years to determine one's preferred learning style. More recently, the concept of a specific preferred or more effective learning style has fallen a little out of favor with educators, since supporting evidence for it is somewhat lacking (Hussman & O'Loughlin, 2019; Pashler, McDaniel, Rohrer, & Bjork, 2009). For example, some evidence suggests that learners use a mixture of learning styles irrespective of their preference, and that the style or styles they use in the classroom may differ from those they use during self-directed study (Hussman & O'Loughlin, 2019). Furthermore, assessment outcomes suggest that use of a preferred learning style doesn't always ensure optimum performance (Hussman & O'Loughlin, 2019). For example, a learner who prefers a kinesthetic learning style may actually perform better on an exam if they instead use a read-write style to prepare for it; indeed, there are examples of learners using a specific style when studying for an assessment task that may not be their preferred style as measured by the VARK questionnaire. Hence, although popular, ascertaining the preferred learning style of your learners may have limited merit.

# UNDERSTANDING LEARNER STRENGTHS AND NEEDS

Gathering information about learners can take various forms, but in this context, it refers specifically to identifying the various aspects of learner variability discussed previously—including demographic information and details relating to how learners approach and engage with learning in the most effective way—particularly by addressing the four aforementioned categories: learning attitudes and mindset; interest and learning needs; social and emotional learning; and cultural relevance and perspectives.

You can then incorporate the information you gather with these tools into a summary of learner strengths and needs. There is no single, optimum way of summarizing this information, and no standard template. Therefore, I encourage you to create your own based on the information you feel is most relevant to supporting your learners.

You'll find a sample summary of learner strengths and needs in Table 3-1. Notice that the summary includes sections for both demographic information and sources of learning information. This may include information you gather from questionnaires, diagnostic assessments, or even one-on-one discussions with your learners. It might even include a grade profile or entry qualifications or points. It's up to you what you include. Next is a section where you can record information relating to each of the four learner variability categories, followed by a section for assessment and instructional considerations based on all the previous information. Notice how the assessment and instructional considerations broadly map to the three UDL principles: engagement, representation, and action and expression. Note that this is just an example and not necessarily what you *should* do; it's included only to stimulate ideas.

You may be thinking that there's no way you have the time to create a profile with so much detail for every learner you teach, and that's understandable. As an alternative approach, you could get the learners to construct their own learner summary sheet. In fact, it could represent an introductory formative task that you assign them. As another idea, you could create a more general summary of the learning groups that you teach—with an overview of key demographic information and information relating to learner variability—so that you're aware of any general trends when planning instruction. For example, you might note that 40 percent of your class find the English language challenging due to their cultural background, or that 15 percent have a specific learning difference, or that 70 percent have no previous learning experience with the topic. This approach is usually used for large class sizes, and in such circumstances, it can be helpful to use one of the predetermined tools on learning preferences. However, if you'd like to try creating your own profile, the process is detailed in Figure 3-1.

TABLE 3-1. Sample Learner Summary Sheet

| Name: _____ | Date: |
|---|---|
| Age: _____ | |
| Course: _____ | |
| Level: _____ | |

| Sources of Information |
|---|
| *[List sources of information used to compile this learner summary here. Note dates when information has been compiled, including the date of any diagnostic assessment.]* |

| Findings from Information Sources: Strengths, Areas of Need, Preferences ||||
|---|---|---|---|
| Current achievement level, learning skills, learning habits, readiness for and motivation to learn | Learning preferences and needs, interests, task preferences, assessment preferences | Social and emotional strengths/needs, individual/group working preferences | Cultural/racial perspectives and experiences, key cultural perspectives to consider |

| Instruction and Assessment |||
|---|---|---|
| Considerations for instructional strategies | Considerations for assessment | Learning resources and support |

**FIGURE 3-1.** "The Process for Developing a Learner" summary sheet. Adapted from the Ontario Ministry of Education (2013).

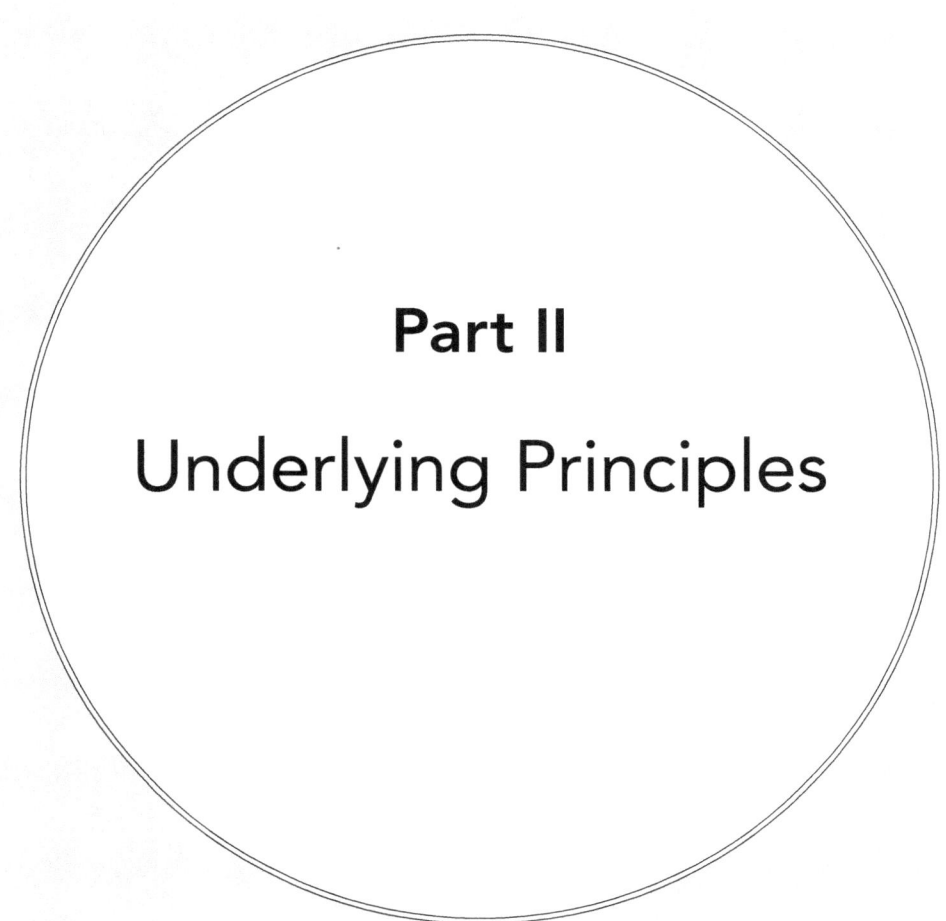

# Part II

# Underlying Principles

# 4

## The Meaning of Mastery

As discussed in Chapter 2, a central purpose of UDL is to support learners to become expert learners. Part of becoming an expert learner is being able to apply a range of practical—and more important, cognitive—skills to the content of learning. A useful tool for this is Bloom's taxonomy (Bloom, Engelhart, Furst, Hill, & Krathwohl, 1956), a framework for classifying learning objectives into different levels or hierarchies of complexity and specificity. It includes three different domains—cognitive, affective, and psychomotor—and as a result is quite involved; there's a lot to get your head around. From a learning and teaching perspective, we tend to focus our attention mostly on the cognitive domain, which has been exceptionally influential in terms of how educators (including those in higher education) create and structure curricula, learning outcomes or goals, activities, and assessments. The original cognitive domain of Bloom's taxonomy is shown in Figure 4-1.

Essentially, the cognitive domain is a hierarchy of cognitive skills, increasing in complexity from bottom to top. We often refer to the skills at the bottom as *lower-order thinking skills*, and those at the top as *higher-order thinking skills*. The skills at the top require greater *cognitive processing*—the ability to put information to work—than the lower-order skills at the bottom. It should come as no surprise, then, that mastering higher-order thinking skills requires more practice and more support than mastering lower-order thinking skills.

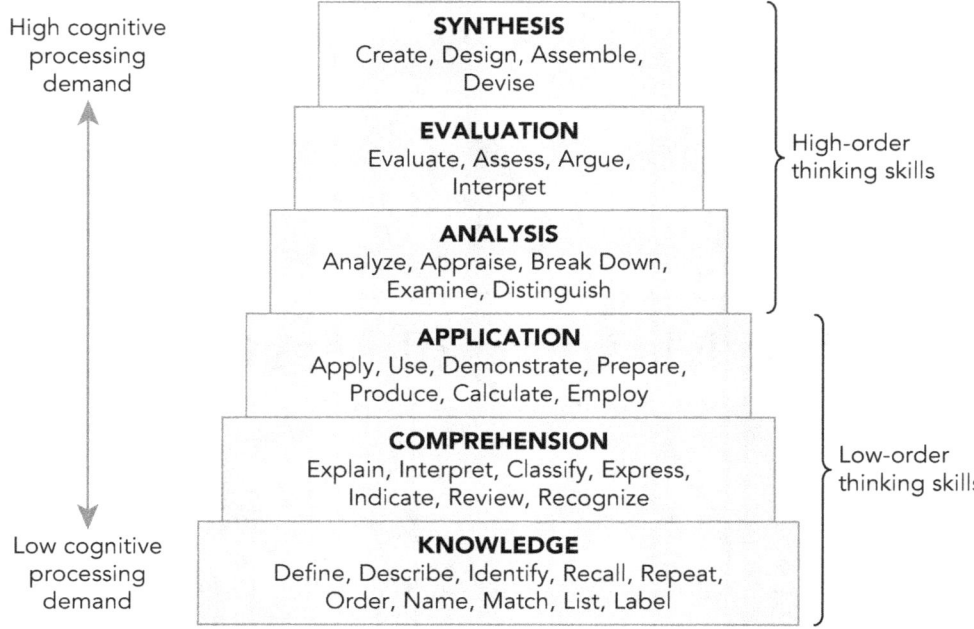

**FIGURE 4-1.** Bloom's taxonomy (Bloom, 1956)

It is sometimes said that a learner has only truly learned about a topic once they are able to apply all the skills in the taxonomy. Accordingly, many teacher training materials say that for a learner to truly understand a topic, they must be able to demonstrate all the skills in Bloom's taxonomy in relation to that topic. The lower levels of the taxonomy are sometimes described as representing *surface* or *rote* learning, and the higher-order skills as representing *deep* or *meaningful* learning (Meyer, 2002; Petty, 2014). I often use the example of Newton's third law when explaining this idea. I could teach my two-year-old daughter to recite Newton's third law: "For every action, there is an equal and opposite reaction." To an extent, she would have some understanding at the *knowledge* (bottom) level of the taxonomy because she knows what to say when I ask her to recite the law; in essence, I'm asking her to *define* the law, which is one of the verbs associated with the knowledge level. However, she would be unable to answer questions about Newton's third law or solve problems with it, because both would require higher-order thinking skills. Thus, we might say her knowledge of the law is at the surface level rather than the deep level. This example also shows us that just because a learner can describe or define something does not mean they understand it deeply.

Bloom's original cognitive domain of the taxonomy significantly influenced teaching and instructional design for roughly 50 years until it was revised in 2001 by Anderson and Krathwohl (2001). The main difference in the revision concerns the position of knowledge within the taxonomy. One of the weaknesses of the original model, as Bloom himself noted, was the important difference between the knowledge level and the other five levels. For example, comprehension, application, analysis, synthesis, and evaluation are intellectual/thinking skills that can be applied to and interact with different types of knowledge. In this sense, knowledge itself isn't an intellectual or cognitive skill but rather something to which intellectual skills are applied, a distinction that the revised taxonomy acknowledges. The updated cognitive domain of the taxonomy is split into six cognitive processes or skills (Figure 4-2), which can be applied to four different types of knowledge: factual, conceptual, procedural, and metacognitive (Table 4-1). These revised cognitive processes or intellectual skills are intended to reflect how they can be applied to different types of knowledge. There is also some repositioning of levels. For example, synthesis (called *creating* in the revised taxonomy) and evaluation have swapped positions to more accurately convey the cognitive function required of them (that is, creating is a more difficult cognitive task than evaluating).

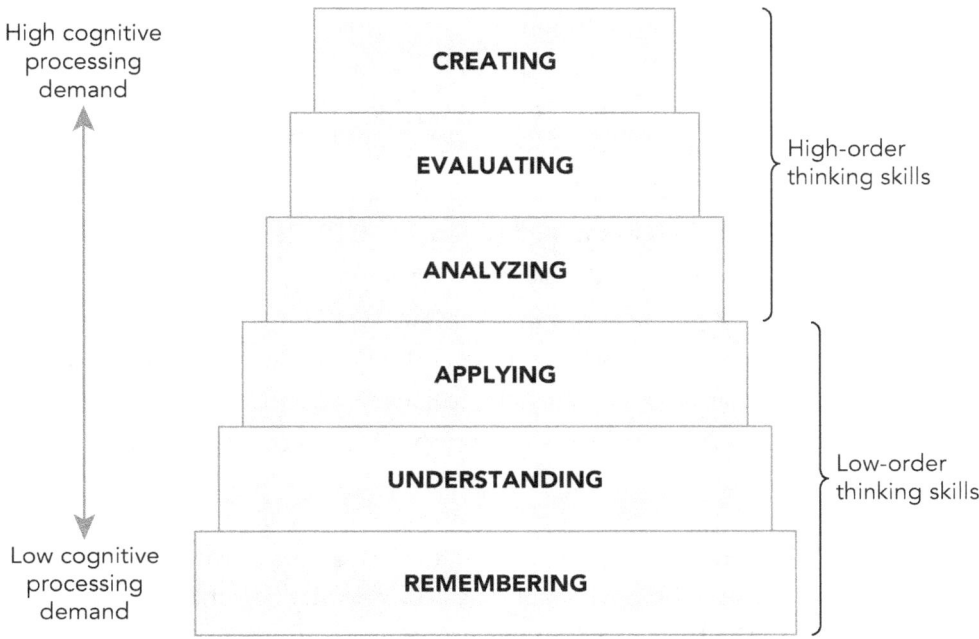

**FIGURE 4-2.** Revised Bloom's taxonomy (Anderson & Krathwohl, 2001)

**TABLE 4-1.** Intersection of Knowledge Dimensions and Cognitive Processes in the Revised Bloom's Taxonomy (Anderson & Krathwohl, 2001)

| COGNITIVE PROCESSES | | | | | | |
|---|---|---|---|---|---|---|
| Knowledge Dimensions | Remembering | Understanding | Applying | Analyzing | Evaluating | Creating |
| Factual | List | Summarize | Classify | Order | Rank | Combine |
| Conceptual | Describe | Interpret | Experiment | Explain | Assess | Plan |
| Procedural | Tabulate | Predict | Calculate | Differentiate | Conclude | Compose |
| Metacognitive | Identify | Execute | Construct | Achieve | Action | Actualize |

Not all educators are fans of the revised taxonomy, and it's certainly not the be-all and end-all of learning and teaching. However, it reminds us that learning isn't just about knowing lots of content—it's also about what learners can *do* with that content. As per the taxonomy's various levels, it's important for learners to be able to comprehend, apply, analyze, evaluate, and even create with content, especially in higher education, since being able to use content cognitively is one of the key characteristics that makes the learning "higher." Therefore, the taxonomy can be an extremely useful way of reminding higher education teachers to avoid stuffing their curricula with more and more content, which is generally what's happened in higher education over the years. Perhaps this is no surprise, given that the main job of a teacher in higher education has traditionally been to transmit content.

Mastering each of the skills in Bloom's taxonomy and attaining true understanding or deep learning has important implications for UDL, because it directly reflects part of the central aim of UDL: supporting the development of expert learners (CAST, 2018). For example, one part of being an expert learner, as discussed in Chapter 2, is being able to master content, which is effectively being able to demonstrate all of the skills in Bloom's taxonomy in relation to a topic. Hence, a good starting point for developing mastery over learning content, with any topic, is to master each of Bloom's skills.

**PAUSE AND THINK** Do you make sure that your learners develop the higher-order thinking skills in Bloom's taxonomy? How do you currently include the development of the higher-order thinking skills into your teaching sessions?

# PRACTICE MAKES PERMANENT

Mastering any skill requires regular practice. Cognitive skills are no different in this regard. If a learner wants to develop their ability to analyze, for example, then it pays to practice analysis regularly.

We've all heard the phrase "practice makes perfect." Unfortunately, it's not true. In reality, "practice makes permanent"—when we practice something, it changes our brain's neurological circuits, which in turn makes the habit permanent. The benefit is that eventually, a new and unfamiliar action or skill can become embedded in our subconscious and carried out automatically. However, this process may also pose some drawbacks. For example, what happens if our practice wasn't correct in the first place? What if we never quite understood what analysis is or how to do it correctly, and as a result we repeatedly practiced it the wrong way? Our incorrect understanding and subsequent application of the skill will have become a permanent habit.

The fact that cognitive skills can be misunderstood and learned incorrectly is a good reminder of the persuasiveness of *constructivism*, the theory that we construct our own understanding of any given idea, topic, or concept based on what we already know about it. Constructivism is based on the ideas of Ausubel (1978), who stated that what the learner already knows is the most important influence on learning. Thus, when learning about our learners and trying to understand their variability, it's exceptionally helpful if we learn what they already know—or more critically, what they *don't* know—about the topics we will teach them.

Unfortunately, our construction of understanding can sometimes be incorrect and require some modification. Modifying our understanding is essentially driven by feedback, so if feedback is lacking or inadequate in any way, then modification can be problematic and our learners won't learn skills correctly. For these reasons, teachers are critical in supporting the learning of all of Bloom's skills, but particularly the higher-order ones—to explain and demonstrate important higher-order thinking skills and also to provide feedback on learners' attempts to apply them correctly. This is sometimes known as *feedback-corrected practice* (Petty, 2014) and directly reflects checkpoint 8.4 in the CAST UDL Guidelines (2018): "increase mastery-oriented feedback." Mastery-oriented feedback is covered in more detail in Chapter 12.

As mentioned at the beginning of this chapter, higher education is unfortunately a little obsessed with subject knowledge or content. This is perhaps unsurprising since the job of an academic is essentially to be a subject matter expert. However, with the ever-increasing focus on lifelong learning, transferability of skills, and employability, we need to help learners develop more than just content or subject knowledge. We must support them to develop their cognitive abilities. Cognitive skills, especially the higher-order ones, are transferable to different contexts, whereas content might not always be. For example, in a former life, I was an exercise physiologist, and I have undergraduate and postgraduate degrees in exercise physiology. However, I never use the content I learned in those programs in my current job as an educational developer. Instead, I use Bloom's skills, particularly the higher-order ones, all the time, as I am constantly required to analyze, evaluate, and synthesize. This is why we must emphasize cognitive skill development when we teach. Our learners will benefit substantially in the long run. We must also emphasize the processes of developing and applying those higher-order cognitive skills and point out their transferability so that learners can apply them in different contexts, particularly their future career. This kind of approach shares some similarities with the *Surface, Deep, and Transfer* model of learning (Hattie et al., 2016), which will be discussed in a little more detail in Chapter 7.

**PAUSE AND THINK** How do you currently find out how much your learners already know about a topic you're about to teach them? Do you make the effort to find out at all? If not, what could you do to find out?

# 5

# Roadmap for Teaching

An effective way to support mastery of Bloom's skills is to apply the *Roadmap for Teaching*, which consists of four critical elements that a teacher should include when embarking upon delivering a block of learning. A *block* of learning in this context is all of the learning and teaching activity that supports the learning of a given topic or content area. (A block, as described in this book, should not be confused with *block teaching* or *immersive scheduling*, which refers to studying one unit or module at a time during a condensed time period [Nerantzi & Chatzidamianos, 2020].) The four critical elements of the Roadmap for Teaching are learning outcomes or goals; learning activities; evaluation activities; and opportunities for feedback (see Figure 5-1).

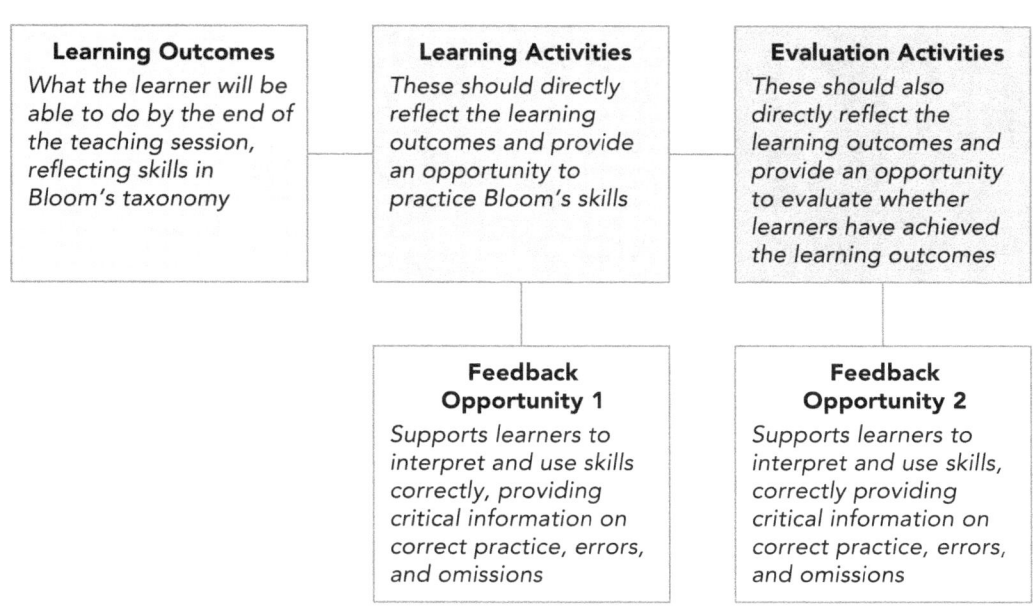

FIGURE 5-1. The Roadmap for Teaching

The Roadmap for Teaching shares similarities with Meyer et al.'s (2014) approach to intentional curriculum design, which consists of goals, assessments, methods, and materials. Goals in Meyer et al.'s model are the same as learning outcomes. Methods are encapsulated in the learning, evaluation, and feedback activities in the roadmap, since it will principally be the teacher providing these things as part of their teaching. Finally, assessments are reflected in evaluation activities in the Roadmap for Teaching. Materials are the missing component in the roadmap, though the expectation is that these will be inherent within each other component; however, if it helps, you could add materials as a wraparound element underpinning the whole model as seen in Figure 5-2.

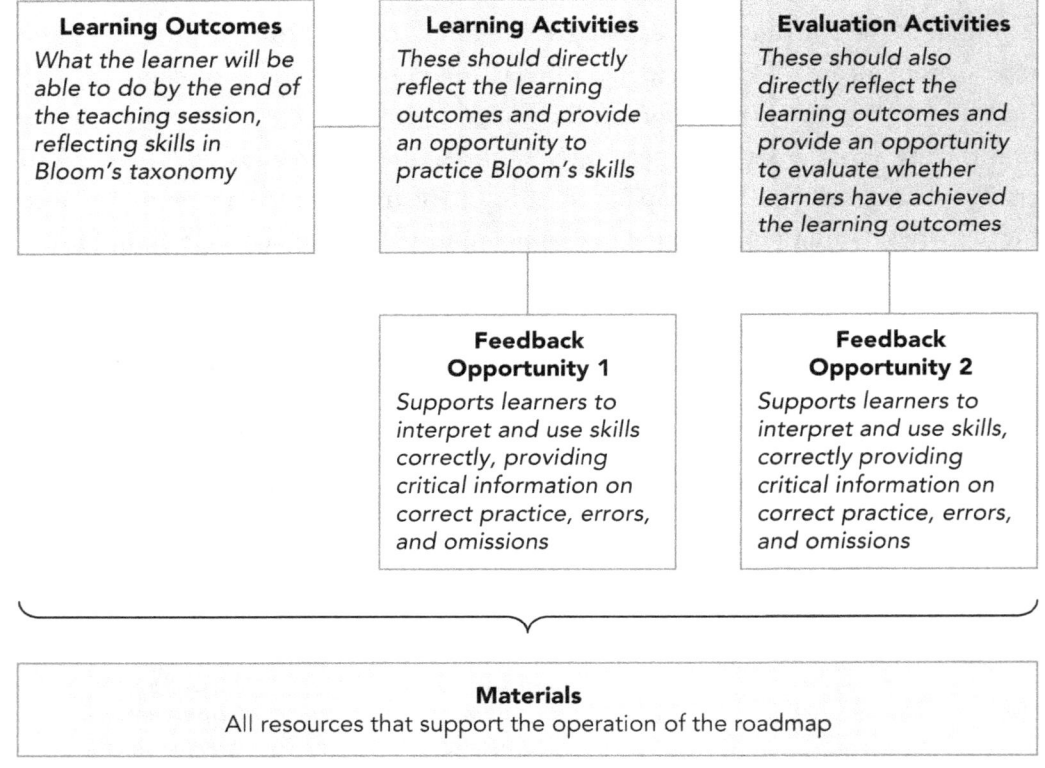

**FIGURE 5-2.** The Roadmap for Teaching including the Materials element

A critical difference between the Roadmap for Teaching and other models of instructional design is the deliberate and intentioned positioning of feedback as part of the instructional experience. As will become apparent, feedback is vitally important to the mastery of all skills, especially cognitive skills. Unfortunately, despite its importance, considerations about where feedback fits into the instructional experience are often nonexistent or at best limited to discussions about summative assessment processes. To remedy this, the Roadmap for Teaching tries to deliberately get educators thinking about how they can include feedback in instructional experiences.

Implementing the Roadmap for Teaching and its individual elements effectively is intentional design in action. We have a clear roadmap that includes where we want our learners to go (learning goals/outcomes) and how we will get them there (learning activities, evaluation activities, feedback).

When you are thinking about how to implement UDL in practice, it is best to begin with intentional design aspects such as the Roadmap for Teaching. You might be tempted to begin by trying to fit the UDL Guidelines directly into your practice, but this often results in a number of challenges—a view shared by Black and Moore (2019). The UDL Guidelines consist of 31 checkpoints split into nine sub-guidelines, spanning the three UDL principles. To fit all of this information into practice at all times is unrealistic and thus might be overwhelming for some (Black & Moore, 2019). As a result, rather than being encouraged by UDL, teachers might be turned off by the prospect of "shoehorning" the guidelines into their practice. Second, applying the guidelines directly to practice may result in some teachers arbitrarily selecting the checkpoints that they recognize or are familiar with. In such circumstances, some may claim that they're already doing UDL (Black & Moore, 2019) and so don't need to develop their practice further.

Essentially, using the Roadmap for Teaching is about making things easy for yourself. Start with the broad design process by thinking about each part of the roadmap and then layer UDL on from there, one step at a time. The guidelines are an excellent tool, but they're best used to stimulate ideas as part of the intentional design process, rather than being followed rigidly.

## LEARNING OUTCOMES

Learning outcomes are what the learner should know or be able to do, once a block of learning has been completed. Since mastery over learning involves being able to demonstrate Bloom's skills, it's important that learning outcomes reflect the skills in Bloom's taxonomy. For example, if your learners need to be able to master analysis skills, then the learning outcomes set for them should include the word *analysis* or a related verb such as *appraise, break down, examine,* or *distinguish.* A hypothetical learning outcome might state, "By the end of this class, you'll be able to distinguish between the learning theories of constructivism and behaviorism." The point here is that cognitive skills in Bloom's taxonomy are being applied to content, which in this case is represented by the learning theories of constructivism and behaviorism. Creating learning outcomes is covered in more detail in Chapter 9. Some key considerations include the following:

- Is it totally clear what learners are expected to know or be able to do as part of the learning outcomes or goals?

- How are learners expected to achieve the learning outcomes or goals?

- How is achievement of the learning outcomes or goals being evaluated?

- Are there outcomes or goals that support learner metacognition—knowing how to master learning through self-assessment, reflection, peer support, and feedback?

- Will the outcomes or goals challenge the learners?

- Do you know the starting point of your learners in relation to achieving the outcomes or goals? Some learners will have to "travel" further than others to achieve the outcomes or goals.

Learning outcomes are a critical part of UDL learning and teaching practices. A key characteristic of the expert learner is that they are "strategic and goal-directed" (CAST, 2018; Meyer et al., 2014); indeed, UDL is often described as goal-directed learning. For learners to be strategic and goal-directed, they need to have a goal or outcome to aim for. As teachers, we can support this by ensuring that each of our teaching sessions is accompanied by a set of intended learning outcomes or goals. From a UDL perspective, these outcomes must be a prominent part of the learning process, as described in checkpoint 8.1 in the CAST UDL Guidelines (2018), "heighten salience of goals and objectives."

Learning outcomes or goals are also critical to the concept of *backward design* (Wiggins & McTighe, 2005), in which we first define the outcomes or goals, stating what we want our learners to know or be able to do. Once we are clear about the outcomes or goals, we then work backward to create the pathways that learners can take to achieve them, defining how we assess or evaluate learning and then thinking about the instructional experience (see Figure 5-3). It's a bit like being able to plan a journey once you know the destination. If you don't know where you're going, you don't know how to get there or how close or how far away you are at any point in the journey. Likewise, outcomes or goals are the destinations that allow us to build critical pathways to learning.

| Establish clear learning goals or outcomes | Design evaluation activities | Design the instructional experience |

**FIGURE 5-3.** Backward design. Adapted from Wiggins and McTighe (2005).

## LEARNING ACTIVITIES

Learning activities are what the learners *do* in order to learn a topic. The emphasis on the word *do* signifies that learners must learn actively, not passively. Indeed, higher-order thinking skills cannot be learned passively; mastering them requires learning by doing (Race, 2019). Learning activities are a critical part of the pathways that we create to support learners to achieve learning outcomes or goals.

Learning activities should directly reflect the cognitive skills articulated in the learning outcomes or goals. For example, using the previous hypothetical learning outcome, the learning activities should require the learners to actually do some *appraising, breaking down, examining,* and *distinguishing* since analysis-type skills are the cognitive skills the learners are trying to master in relation to content. Thus, learning activities provide an opportunity for learners to practice Bloom's skills. Active practice is, of course, critical in the development and mastery of any skill because practice enables learners to safely make mistakes as well as improve through feedback in a process of trial and error (Race, 2019).

Since the engagement principle of UDL is applied largely through learning and teaching approaches and methods, learning activities are critical to the successful application of the engagement principle, especially the aspect of recruiting interest (hence the need to learn actively rather than passively). This concept is reflected directly in checkpoint 7.2 of the UDL Guidelines in that active participation in learning is central to "optimize relevance, value, and authenticity" (CAST, 2018). Some key considerations for learning activities include the following:

- Are learning activities directly aligned with the learning outcomes or goals?

- Are there options and choices in relation to learning activities that support reduction or removal of barriers?
- Are there opportunities for learners to receive feedback when engaging in learning activities?
- Are there opportunities for learners to provide feedback when engaging in learning activities?
- Does feedback have a mastery orientation?
- Are there opportunities for learners to self-assess or reflect upon their performance during learning activities?

The creation of learning activities is covered in more detail in Chapter 10.

## EVALUATION ACTIVITIES

The only way to know if learners have achieved the learning outcomes or goals set for them is through evaluation. This can be done in a multitude of ways, from simple knowledge-check activities to more complex formative assessment tasks. Irrespective of the form they take, evaluation activities enable teachers to assess whether learners have met learning outcomes or goals and subsequently mastered Bloom's skills. Therefore, evaluation activities should directly reflect the learning outcomes or goals.

Sticking with our previous hypothetical learning outcome, learners would need to be provided with a task that actually gets them to *distinguish* between the learning theories of constructivism and behaviorism, since that is what is articulated in the learning outcome. This relationship between learning outcomes or goals, learning activities, and evaluation activities, known as *constructive alignment* (Biggs & Tang, 2011), directly reflects the UDL aim of developing expert learners who are "strategic and goal-directed" (CAST, 2018) because it's driven by learning outcomes or goals and includes a clear strategy for achieving them. Evaluation activities also directly reflect the UDL principle of action and expression because they represent opportunities for learners to express what they know.

Evaluation activities also support teachers in providing differentiated instruction and feedback. Differentiation essentially means tailoring instruction and feedback to meet individual learning needs to support learners to learn most effectively.

Generally, teachers may differentiate learning content, learning processes, the learning environment and its constituent parts (including materials and resources), and the products of learning (such as evaluation activities themselves or even assessments). For example, a teacher may differentiate content for learners based on their level of understanding of a given topic. In this hypothetical example, the teacher may set some learning activities that span the various levels of Bloom's taxonomy. Learners who have limited prior knowledge or understanding of the topic might be required to undertake activities that reflect the lower levels of Bloom's taxonomy (the lower-order skills), as they must develop the baseline concepts and ideas related to the topic. Conversely, learners with prior knowledge or understanding of the topic might be asked to complete learning activities that reflect higher levels (i.e., higher-order skills) of the taxonomy. The content, tasks, and activities the learners are presented with would reflect their grouping based on prior knowledge and understanding of the topic. Grouping in this way is flexible, and learners may move between groups as their knowledge and understanding changes. Please note this is just a simplified example, rather than a detailed discussion, to illustrate the broad ideas behind differentiation.

Evaluation activities represent a source of information upon which teachers can make decisions about learning and teaching strategies to group learners based on their needs. To an extent, when we provide options and choices in relation to the three UDL principles, we are enabling learners to self-differentiate aspects of their learning experience, even if the groupings themselves have been decided by the teacher. Whatever the learners are doing, regardless of their grouping, they should be participating in a learning experience that has been universally designed with multiple means of engagement, representation, and action and expression. Some key considerations for evaluation activities include the following:

- Are evaluation activities directly aligned with the learning outcomes or goals?
- Are there options and choices in relation to evaluation activities that support reduction or removal of barriers?
- Are there opportunities for learners to receive feedback when engaging in evaluation activities?
- Are there opportunities for learners to provide feedback when engaging in evaluation activities?
- Does feedback have a mastery orientation?

- Are there opportunities for learners to self-assess or reflect upon their performance during evaluation activities?

Evaluation activities are covered in more depth in Chapter 11.

## FEEDBACK

To ensure that learners are correctly interpreting and practicing the cognitive skills articulated in the learning outcomes or goals, you must provide feedback. Feedback can be applied at two points in the Roadmap for Teaching. First, when the learners are engaging in learning activities, you have an opportunity to give feedback on their attempts at the skills articulated in the learning outcomes or goals, which reflects checkpoint 8.4, "increase mastery-oriented feedback" (CAST, 2018), as mentioned earlier. The second feedback opportunity is following completion of evaluation activities. Giving feedback in this way is known as *feedback-corrected practice* (Petty, 2014). Essentially, learners should practice skills with feedback as part of a continuous loop until they have mastered them (Petty, 2014).

Without feedback, learners are unlikely to master these skills. Feedback applied formatively in this way likely plays a very important role in supporting learning (Knight & Yorke, 2003), as well as in keeping learners "at it" to maintain their motivation for learning (Race, 2019). Keeping learners motivated this way relates to the engagement principle and specifically the UDL guideline of "sustaining effort and persistence" (CAST, 2018), which itself is related to increasing mastery-oriented feedback as mentioned earlier. Some key considerations for feedback include the following:

- Are there opportunities for learners to receive feedback when engaging in learning activities and evaluation activities?

- Does feedback possess a mastery orientation?

- Are there opportunities for learners to provide feedback when engaging in learning activities and evaluation activities?

- Are there opportunities for learners to self-assess or reflect upon their performance during learning activities and evaluation activities?

- Are learners encouraged to use feedback to develop long-term learning habits and strategies?

Feedback-corrected practice was mentioned briefly in Chapter 4 and is discussed further in Chapter 10. Mastery-oriented feedback is covered in more detail in Chapter 12.

**PAUSE AND THINK** Think about your teaching sessions. Do you currently include each of the elements of the Roadmap for Teaching? Is there any element that is missing? If so, why? Can you easily include the missing element(s)?

# 6

# What We've Always Done

One thing you may notice about the Roadmap for Teaching is that its implementation relies heavily on the teacher. It's up to the teacher to set clear learning outcomes or goals, plan the learning and evaluation activities, and provide feedback accordingly. Hence, teachers play a critical role in supporting the mastery of Bloom's skills. To a degree, UDL reinvents the teaching role, requiring teachers to become more like learning engineers or learning architects, iteratively designing learning experiences that support all learners to learn effectively. Adopting a UDL approach to teaching means that teachers no longer can just be subject matter experts or pontificators of content, as some might have been in the past. Teachers must be agile, responsive, and flexible facilitators of learning for all learners. Unfortunately, higher education has been quite slow to embrace such ideas.

Traditionally, higher education has operated according to a model in which the teacher largely owns the "what," "why," and "how" of the learning experience, directing what is studied, why it is studied, and how learners learn it. Thus, different learning pathways enabling learners with distinct needs to make choices about their learning haven't always been available, or have been limited to those with special needs. As mentioned in Chapter 1, renowned UDL expert and consultant Katie Novak has used a café analogy to explain this point, likening traditional classrooms to a café that serves only cream or cow's milk. If you want soy, oat, or coconut milk, you either can't have it at all or have to demonstrate that you are lactose intolerant before a special effort is made to meet your needs. We might say, then, that higher education has been quite teacher-centered, rather than learner-centered.

Higher education has also utilized a model in which contact time, or time learners spend with teachers and peers, is predominantly used to support the development of lower-order thinking skills. This usually takes place via the transmission of information in lectures or other didactic teaching situations, during which learners passively absorb information. Subsequently, the expectation has been that learners will mostly develop higher-order thinking skills for themselves during self-directed study time. Consider the expression that a learner "reads" for a degree. I still remember my first day at university, when my new roommate asked me what I was "reading," meaning what subject was I going to be studying. The idea was that teaching staff would provide you with the basic information on a given topic during teaching sessions, which predominantly consisted of lectures, and you tried to make sense of it by studying (reading) the topic in your own time. Seminars supported the "making sense" part of it to an extent, but the general rule was that at least two-thirds of study time should be independent, placing the onus firmly on the learner (Biggs & Tang, 2011). Figure 6-1 illustrates this process, which, despite being an extreme example, makes clear the point that learners have been expected to master Bloom's higher-order thinking skills themselves predominantly during self-directed study time.

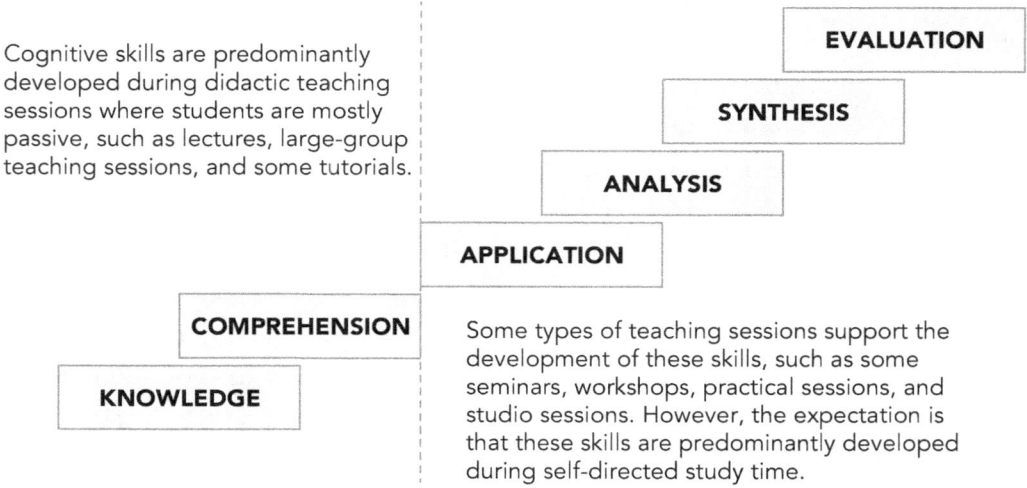

**FIGURE 6-1.** Development of cognitive skills in the traditional higher education teaching model

This model may have worked well at a time when learners in higher education were a largely homogenous group in terms of age, ethnicity, nationality, socioeconomic status, previous educational experiences, entry grades, and the like. Perhaps then it wasn't so problematic for universities to be less accessible, inclusive, flexible, and responsive to the needs of diverse learners, because the learners themselves were not as diverse as they are now. As discussed in Chapter 2, learners in higher education have never been more diverse than they are today. Learner variability is covered in Chapter 3.

The diversity of today's learners means that we can't assume the old one-size-fits-all approach will support all learners in mastering the content of their learning, particularly the higher-order thinking skills that are so critical to mastery. It also means that we as teachers must be more responsive to diverse learner needs, spending more of our time making learning accessible, inclusive, and equitable than we did in the past. In short, the old model will not support the development of learning expertise in the majority of cases because learners are more diverse and thus possess greater variability than in the past.

This idea represents a major paradigm shift in the way in which higher education has played out for generations, and some educators are uneasy with the change in the status quo. However, for those of us with a passion for and interest in teaching, this is great news because it places far greater emphasis on the importance of teaching and teachers in higher education.

As the level of learner diversity increases, so too does the need for a UDL approach to learning, teaching, and assessment. If we're interested in our learners mastering their learning but recognize that each will achieve that mastery in a slightly different way, then it is up to us as teachers to ensure that our practices reflect the principles of UDL.

**PAUSE AND THINK** How do you currently use the time you spend with your learners? Are you predominantly delivering content through lectures? Are you supporting them to learn experientially in practical situations such as lab sessions or workshops? Are you setting tasks for them?

# 7

# The Cheese Sandwich

So far, we've seen how Bloom's taxonomy can support learners in mastering the content of their learning as part of becoming an expert learner, as well as how we can make mastery an intentional part of instructional design by applying the Roadmap for Teaching. Now we'll turn our attention to a concept known as the Cheese Sandwich (Merry, 2019), which combines all the thinking behind content mastery and the Roadmap for Teaching into a single instructional design approach. Critically, the Cheese Sandwich approach to supporting learning recognizes the importance of teacher and peer support to learners developing higher-order thinking skills, and thus refocuses how the time that learners spend with their teachers and peers is used.

As covered in the previous chapter, rather than relying largely on self-directed learning to support the development of higher-order thinking skills, in the Cheese Sandwich the emphasis is placed on the time learners spend with their teachers and peers. Conversely, development of the lower-order thinking skills can take place during self-directed study time.

## COVERING ENTIRE TOPICS

Effectively, the Cheese Sandwich represents a block of learning, which, as Chapter 5 discussed, constitutes all of the learning and teaching activity that supports the learning of a given topic or content area. A block of learning has an associated set of learning outcomes or goals, which can be achieved across the whole block. In this regard, the Cheese Sandwich helps to solve the age-old teaching conundrum of trying to fit content delivery, learning activities, evaluation activities, and feedback all into a single session of teaching to support the achievement of given learning outcomes or goals.

In the Cheese Sandwich, the process of learners achieving learning outcomes or goals is extended across three phases: 1) self-directed learning that happens before learners learn with direct support from teachers and peers; 2) learning that is directly supported by teachers and peers; and 3) self-directed learning that happens after learners learn with direct support from teachers and peers. This affords teachers an extended opportunity to fit content delivery, learning activities, evaluation activities, and feedback into the instructional experience. The time learners spend with teachers and peers is "sandwiched" between periods of self-directed study, giving this approach its name (see Table 7-1).

**TABLE 7-1.** The Cheese Sandwich Approach to Supporting Learning

| ACHIEVEMENT OF LEARNING OUTCOMES CONTAINING BLOOM'S SKILLS—EMPHASIS ON TRANSFERABILITY | | |
|---|---|---|
| **Pre-time with teachers and peers** | **Time with teachers and peers** | **Post-time with teachers and peers** |
| Self-directed study | Teacher/peer-supported study | Self-directed study |
| Primarily for content engagement | Recap of content and key learning points covered during self-directed study | Opportunities to revisit in-session learning |
| Development of lower-order cognitive skills through low-demand activities | Primarily for supporting higher-order cognitive skills development | Evaluation to test capability to apply higher-order cognitive skills through formative assessment reflecting learning outcomes |
| Opportunities for self-assessment (feedback) of lower-order cognitive skills reflecting learning outcomes | Explanation and/or demonstration of higher-order skills | Opportunities for self-assessment |
| Opportunity for reflection on progress | Active collaborative practice of higher-order skills (active learning with peers) reflecting learning outcomes | Opportunity to reflect on progress |

| ACHIEVEMENT OF LEARNING OUTCOMES CONTAINING BLOOM'S SKILLS—EMPHASIS ON TRANSFERABILITY | | |
|---|---|---|
| Pre-time with teachers and peers | Time with teachers and peers | Post-time with teachers and peers |
| Opportunity for learners to ask questions, seek clarification, and give feedback | E-tivities reflecting learning outcomes | Opportunities for learners to ask questions, seek clarification, and give feedback |
| | Feedback-corrected practice (mastery-oriented feedback) | |
| | Active practice of higher-order skills should be repeated in this phase | |
| | Opportunity to reflect on progress | |
| | Opportunity for learners to ask questions, seek clarification, and give feedback | |

# THE IMPORTANCE OF TEACHER AND PEER SUPPORT

The most important part of any sandwich is its filling. Hence, the time learners spend with their teachers and peers represents the "cheese" in the Cheese Sandwich (center column in Table 7-1) because it is during this time that learners can be best supported to master those all-important higher-order thinking skills by engaging in active, collaborative learning and evaluation activities supplemented with feedback. The time learners spend with teachers and peers could be broadly described as a "teaching session," but the nature of that session is nonspecific. For example, it could be a seminar, practical, or workshop. Regardless of what it is called, it represents a time when learners are together in a physical or virtual space with their teachers and their peers working on developing higher-order thinking skills in a supported way.

As you can see in Table 7-1, the cheese portion of the Cheese Sandwich encompasses learning and teaching approaches that reflect many ideas from the cognitivist and constructivist schools of learning, with learners required to undertake active learning activities and tasks that are challenging, involve applying higher-order thinking skills, and are supplemented by continual feedback on the proficiency with which those skills are applied. Activities may involve discussion, questioning, problem solving, defending or challenging a position, or implementing a strategy, to name a few possibilities. The point is that the activities are active, collaborative (undertaken with and supported by peers), and aligned to the learning outcomes or goals, and require learners to think deeply about what they are doing and reflect on how well they are learning. You'll also notice in the cheese portion of Table 7-1 that learners are provided with regular opportunities to clarify their understanding by asking questions, often in ways that allow peer collaboration, content sharing, and raising of ideas. Peer support through sharing and collaboration is a key ingredient of the Cheese Sandwich.

## CHANGING THE NATURE OF SELF-DIRECTED LEARNING

The "slices of bread" in the Cheese Sandwich (the left and right columns of Table 7-1) represent what happens before and after the time that learners spend with their teachers and peers, with a focus on self-directed study. At these times, learners engage with content in a variety of ways, including the use of prerecorded multimedia options such as videos, screencasts, and podcasts. Supplementary materials such as presentation slides, reading resources, and summary information are also included to support self-directed study in these phases. The slices of bread are also when learners practice important lower-order cognitive skills, largely at the knowledge and comprehension levels, as well as when teachers evaluate those skills through various tasks and knowledge-check activities. Since effective learning designs are iterative, requiring continual learner feedback, opportunities for learners to give feedback are inherent within the Cheese Sandwich at each phase. During self-directed study, learners predominantly give feedback on learning resources and materials and **self-directed learning tasks and activities**, including knowledge-check activities.

## ACCESSIBLE LEARNING

When learners are together with their teachers and peers **as part of the cheese portion of the Cheese Sandwich, didactic teaching elements are minimized**—limited to recapping important content and key learning points addressed during self-directed study, with the emphasis placed firmly on learning actively through feedback-corrected practice. All learning covered when learners and teachers are together is made available to review, replay, or revisit through various mechanisms, including video recordings of any didactic teaching elements. Videos should contain closed captions, a transcript, media alternative transcript where necessary, and standard and extended audio descriptions where necessary. Notes and summaries can also be used for learners to review or revisit learning. Ideally, these should be provided electronically in flexible formats so that learners can adjust the layout, font size, style, and color. If other resources are linked, it is helpful to avoid phrases such as "click here" in favor of descriptive text hyperlinks such as "Find articles by searching the university catalog" or similar. Notes and summaries in hard-copy (printed) format should use a sans serif font (e.g., Arial or Verdana), with a font size of 12–14, line spacing of 1.5, and left justification. Bold text, rather than italics or underlining, should be used to emphasize important words, phrases, or sections. Also use strong contrast between the background and text, such as dark-colored text on a pastel background (cream, light yellow, etc.). Red and green should never be contrasted with each other. Sometimes notes and summaries may contain photos, tables, or figures, or such resources may be provided in stand-alone fashion to support learning. In each case, it is important to use alternative text on any photos, images, tables, or figures. Graphic organizers and many other types of resources can also be used to support learning, always in modifiable formats. In addition, be sure to share all learning materials—including handouts, activity instructions, links to websites, background information, and briefs for evaluation/assessment—with all learners in modifiable formats ahead of the block of learning to be studied, ensuring that all learners receive key information and resources related to their learning in a timely fashion and adhering to the previously described accessibility considerations. In other words, provide learners with everything they require to support their learning of a topic in advance of it being studied.

## IT STARTS WITH DESIGN

The Cheese Sandwich is the vehicle for implementing the Roadmap for Teaching covered in Chapter 5. Whether learning is self-directed or supported by teachers and peers, the Cheese Sandwich includes the four critical elements of the Roadmap for Teaching (outcomes or goals, learning activities, evaluation activities, and feedback), as indicated by the bolded cells in Table 7-2.

**TABLE 7-2.** The Four Critical Elements of the Roadmap for Teaching Within the Cheese Sandwich

| ACHIEVEMENT OF LEARNING OUTCOMES CONTAINING BLOOM'S SKILLS—EMPHASIS ON TRANSFERABILITY | | |
|---|---|---|
| **Pre-time with teachers and peers** | **Time with teachers and peers** | **Post-time with teachers and peers** |
| Self-directed study | Teacher/peer-supported study | Self-directed study |
| Primarily for content engagement | Recap of content and key learning points covered during self-directed study | Opportunities to revisit in-session learning |
| **Development of lower-order cognitive skills through low-demand activities** | Primarily for supporting higher-order cognitive skills development | **Evaluation to test capability to apply higher-order cognitive skills through formative assessment reflecting learning outcomes** |
| **Opportunities for self-assessment (feedback) of lower-order cognitive skills reflecting learning outcomes** | Explanation and/or demonstration of higher-order skills | **Opportunities for self-assessment** |
| Opportunity for reflection on progress | **Active collaborative practice of higher-order skills (active learning with peers) reflecting learning outcomes** | Opportunity to reflect on progress |
| Opportunity for learners to ask questions, seek clarification, and give feedback | E-tivities reflecting learning outcomes | Opportunities for learners to ask questions, seek clarification, and give feedback |
| | **Feedback-corrected practice (mastery-oriented feedback)** | |
| | **Active practice of higher-order skills should be repeated in this phase** | |
| | Opportunity to reflect on progress | |
| | Opportunity for learners to ask questions, seek clarification, and give feedback | |

# CHEESE SANDWICH PRINCIPLES

The Cheese Sandwich is based on these five important principles:

1. Learners should be supported to become expert learners by achieving mastery over their learning.

2. The role of the teacher (lecturer) is to support learners in developing mastery, not just deliver content.

3. Learners are more likely to master learning in the presence of teachers and peers.

4. Learners are more likely to master learning if they learn actively rather than passively.

5. Learners are more likely to master learning if their learning experience is customizable to their preferences (engagement, representation, action and expression).

Implementing each principle is critical to the effective operation of the Cheese Sandwich, and failure to do so will produce suboptimal results.

# FLIPPED LEARNING

Principle 3 is particularly important, since it encapsulates the very essence of the Cheese Sandwich: Learners need support from their teachers and peers to master their learning. In this respect, the Cheese Sandwich shares critical elements of *flipped learning* (Bergmann & Sams, 2012). I get quite annoyed when the topic of flipped learning is discussed, because often the conversation turns to how we can best use videos in our teaching sessions. Flipped learning isn't about using videos in teaching sessions—it's about how the time learners spend with their teachers and peers can be most effectively used to support learning. Of course, videos and other multimedia applications can be used to support learning as part of a flipped approach, particularly in terms of content delivery. As mentioned previously, the use of several prerecorded multimedia options, such as videos, screencasts, and podcasts, is encouraged as part of content delivery and for replaying, reviewing, or recapping important learning in the Cheese Sandwich, with all multimedia resources made available for learners to access on their own devices. Prerecorded, self-directed learning materials are limited to 20 minutes in duration and include built-in activities and knowledge checks to help maintain learner focus. Furthermore, the use of supplementary supporting materials, such as learning glossaries, is encouraged to support familiarity with and subsequent learning of new and unfamiliar terms. As noted earlier, all further learning materials (handouts, activity instructions, links to websites, background information, and briefs for evaluation/assessment) also must be shared in modifiable formats before learners come together in a physical or virtual space with their teachers and peers. Despite the centrality of multimedia and other technological innovations within the Cheese Sandwich, however, the emphasis is firmly on how we can effectively use the time learners spend with their teachers and peers to develop their higher-order cognitive capabilities, including metacognitive capabilities. Technological innovation is used intentionally to support these aims, without being an aim in itself.

The critical question that the Cheese Sandwich attempts to address is: At what point in the learning process do learners most need support from teachers and peers? In the Cheese Sandwich, the point at which learners begin to engage in higher-order thinking is when they most need support from teachers and peers, because typically, the higher-order skills are more difficult to master and require more support. For example, targeted instruction can be delivered to individual learners or groups of learners who are learning higher-order cognitive skills, and those who find learning the skills difficult can be supported more readily, while those who make sense of the learning more quickly can be stretched and challenged through differentiated instruction. The teacher has the opportunity to engage with individual learners about their understanding as they work independently or in small groups. In this model, the teacher is engaged in a continual cycle of checking for understanding, immediately determining each learner's level of understanding, and providing feedback to support the modification of their understanding.

Shifting the development of the lower-order skills in Bloom's taxonomy into self-directed study time means that learners can use the support of their teachers and peers to help them spend more time developing the more cognitively demanding higher-order skills. It is critical that learners practice and develop higher-order thinking skills if they are to learn deeply. The use of lots of quick and easy tasks requiring lower-order skills will support only surface learning, not the use of learning content and the development of deep learning. It can be tempting to set lots of low-order tasks when we teach, since they provide almost immediate payoff in that learners can master them relatively quickly. However, on their own, they do not really support mastery over learning and subsequent expert or deep learning, as discussed in Chapter 4.

# CLIMBING BLOOM'S TAXONOMY AND LEARNING DEEPLY

Although we should be aware of the limitations of relying on lower-order tasks, also keep in mind that in a given learning scenario learners should master lower-order skills before they develop the higher-order ones. Consider a simple example. In one of my introductory teaching courses for novice higher education teachers, one of the learning outcomes is "By the end of the course you will be able to create clear, realistic, and measurable learning outcomes." To *create* in Bloom's taxonomy is a higher-order skill. However, before the course participants can create their clear, realistic, and measurable learning outcomes, they need to know what a clear, realistic, and measurable learning outcome *is*. This would involve the *knowledge* and *comprehension* levels of Bloom's taxonomy—both lower-order skills. Hence, the learners need some lower-order skills (knowledge and comprehension) before they can apply higher-order ones (creation). This is why we're encouraged to set tasks that, as Geoff Petty states, enable learners to climb Bloom's taxonomy like a ladder (Petty, 2014). The Cheese Sandwich does this by positioning the lower-order skills within the slices of bread, particularly the pre-contact-time slice. Learners then move on to the higher-order skills during the cheese (contact-time) phase, gaining support from their teachers and peers.

The Cheese Sandwich is built on the belief that higher-order cognitive skills can be mastered through practice. Learning in this sense is not about innate ability, but trial and error. As covered in Chapter 4, the more a learner practices the higher-order cognitive skills, receives formative feedback, and incorporates the feedback into their practice, the better they will become at applying the skills.

As stated previously, key ideas from the cognitivist and constructivist schools of learning feature heavily within the Cheese Sandwich approach. For example, the mastery of the cognitive skills in Bloom's taxonomy, especially the higher-order ones, is a central feature of the Cheese Sandwich. Mastering those all-important higher-order thinking skills through the use of tasks in which those skills are applied supports deep (Petty, 2014) or meaningful (Meyer, 2002) learning, as opposed to surface or rote learning (Meyer, 2002). These tasks involve learning by doing or active learning, requiring learners to make a "construct," receive in-the-moment formative feedback on their application of the skills, and then incorporate that feedback into their practice. This cycle of feedback-corrected practice, where the emphasis is placed on what the learner is doing rather than what the teacher is doing, continues until the learner masters the skills. Feedback-corrected practice is covered in more detail in Chapter 12.

## CUSTOMIZABLE LEARNING

Principle 5 of the Cheese Sandwich states that learners are more likely to master learning if their learning experience is customizable to their preferences. This is where the UDL principles of engagement, representation, and action and expression become critical, and where the UDL Guidelines (CAST, 2018) can be used to stimulate ideas throughout each aspect of the Cheese Sandwich. This is an important point. As Chapter 5 noted, it could be a little overwhelming, not to mention challenging, to try to immediately fit all 31 UDL checkpoints into the design of a Cheese Sandwich–style learning experience. It's better to layer UDL on gradually.

---

### LAYERING ON UDL

Let's consider how to layer UDL on gradually as part of the Cheese Sandwich. Designing an instructional experience using the Cheese Sandwich always begins with the learning outcomes. When considering how to support learners to meet learning outcomes as part of a Cheese Sandwich learning experience, it's useful to split the outcomes into content knowledge and skills (which usually means cognitive skills).

Here's a real example. As noted earlier in the chapter, one of the learning outcomes for my introductory teaching course is "By the end of this course you will be able to create clear, realistic, and measurable learning outcomes." To accomplish this, the learners need some lower-order skills (knowledge and comprehension) before they can apply higher-order ones (creation). Knowing what a clear, realistic, and measurable learning outcome is represents content knowledge. Now I can think of a variety of ways that I could deliver that content knowledge, such as:

- Teacher talk
- A video

- A podcast
- A reading task
- A self-directed learning task

In the Cheese Sandwich, learners usually engage with content before they come to class. Hence, perhaps teacher talk isn't the best way to deliver the content, since it would eat into precious class time. Let's say approximately 20 percent of my class are learners with dyslexia and 40 percent are non-native English speakers (these proportions are not uncommon). Perhaps, then, a reading task completed before class also wouldn't be optimal, since ~60 percent of the learners might find it challenging, thus presenting a barrier to their learning. That's not to say that I shouldn't include reading activities at all, but due to the possible barriers they raise for some learners, it would be useful to provide alternative options. Remember, UDL is about removing and reducing barriers.

Therefore, I might instead create a short video about learning outcomes. I would make sure the video included closed captions, standard and extended audio descriptions where necessary, and a transcript and media alternative transcript where necessary too.

The videos I create are usually prerecorded PowerPoint presentations. I would make sure the slides I use adhere to PowerPoint accessibility considerations in terms of order, language, layout, and the use of tables, figures, and images. As well as making the video itself available to the learners before class, I'd also provide the slides used to make the video in alternative, modifiable formats compatible with screen reading software.

I script my videos, writing my script in the notes sections of each PowerPoint slide. Hence, as well as including a standard written transcript, I would provide another (verbatim) transcript in the slides themselves, corresponding perfectly with the content information presented on each slide. Hyperlinks to further resources would also be included in the slides should learners want to access them for further self-directed learning; this is not compulsory but accommodates learners who perhaps desire more information or a "stretch and challenge." The video is also available to download as a podcast, and all of the above materials (video, slides, podcast, transcript) are made available at least 48 hours before class in the course learning management system (LMS).

> Therefore, the learners may watch the video, listen to the podcast, read the slides or transcript, access the further resources as a self-directed learning task, or do all of the above to support their engagement with the content of their learning. In this way, we're breaking down the learning outcomes into their constituent parts to layer UDL on, providing flexible options. Learners can access the content in a variety of ways.
>
> For guidance on creating accessible videos, podcasts, PowerPoint slides, and Word and PDF documents, please see Chapter 13.

One other note of caution related to applying the UDL principles is that it's not just about providing as many options and choices as possible for each of the three principles—it's about providing options and choices that genuinely reduce or remove barriers to learning for your learners. We're employing thoughtful, intelligent design based on our knowledge of the variability of our learners, the barriers they may face, and our desire to ensure that they are not excluded. Thus, the basis for employing the Cheese Sandwich approach is to first understand the variability of your learners, and then layer UDL on as described.

The options and choices you provide as part of the Cheese Sandwich are influenced by feedback from learners. Notice in Tables 7-1 and 7-2 that each part of the Cheese Sandwich includes opportunities for learners to give feedback to teachers on what has or hasn't helped support their learning. Effective UDL practice is an iterative process in that it requires continual dialogue with learners to help them become expert learners based on where they are right now, not where they were yesterday or last week.

As mentioned in Chapter 3, some sources of variability are constantly changing and consequently difficult to predict. Therefore, we must continually ask our learners about what will help them to achieve learning goals and about their understanding, how they think they're getting on, and what would help them to be successful. We must reflect on all of this information to continually make tweaks and modifications to our approach to supporting our learners. Indeed, reflection is really the starting point of effective UDL practice because it helps us to get into the UDL mindset explored in Chapter 2.

Take a moment to think about the learning outcomes or goals that you set for your learners. Then think about the pathway the learners must move along to achieve those outcomes or goals. Traditionally, higher education has offered only one pathway to learning; everyone gets the same. As a starting point, can you think of one other pathway that learners could navigate to support achievement of learning outcomes or goals? If your content is currently delivered as a lecture, is there another way that it could be delivered? If the learners are required to undertake an individual reading and comprehension task as part of a seminar, is there a different way that they could make sense of the content? Finally, if you assess their knowledge through an essay or exam, is there another way that they could express their knowledge of the content?

As your practice with UDL develops, you'll create multiple pathways to support the achievement of learning goals in your learners. Those pathways will be focused on removing or reducing barriers experienced by your learners based on their variability, as shown in Figure 7-1. Remember, the barrier is never with the learner, but always with the environment; barriers result from the interaction between sources of variability and the learning environment. For example, being a learner with dyslexia is not a barrier. However, giving a lecture in which a learner with dyslexia is required to take extensive notes quickly *is* a barrier. If you expected that learner to then make further sense of the lecture content with various reading and comprehension tasks that they must respond to in writing, you would be adding further barriers. Does this sound familiar? It should, because it has been the way many higher education programs have been delivered for generations. The scenario just described would also erect barriers for learners for whom English is a second language, or anyone who doesn't like to passively absorb content or read.

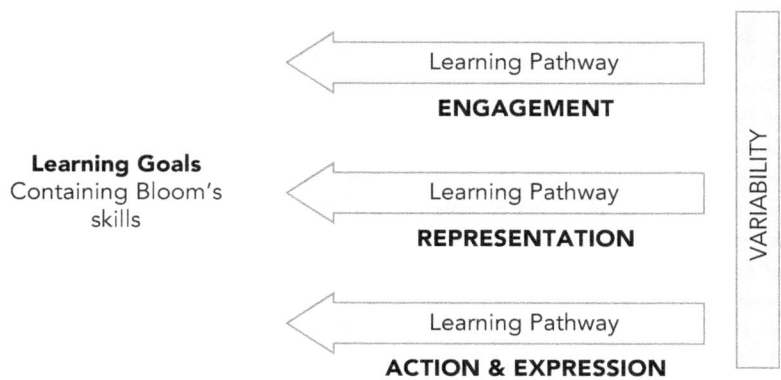

**FIGURE 7-1.** Multiple pathways to achieve learning goals are driven by learner variability.

Reducing the requirement to listen passively, take lots of notes, and read and write extensively would go some way to reducing the aforementioned barriers. Furthermore, do the learning goals really require all that note-taking, reading, and writing to be met effectively? These are the types of questions you must reflect on.

Table 7-3 shows how the UDL principles must be applied to an entire Cheese Sandwich or block of learning to support mastery over the learning within that block. As you can see, teachers must apply multiple means of getting learners interested in learning (engagement) at each stage, as well as multiple types of learning resources (representation). There must also be multiple ways for learners to demonstrate their learning at each stage (action and expression).

**TABLE 7-3.** How the Cheese Sandwich Applies the UDL Principles to Each Stage to Support Learner Mastery Over Learning

| ACHIEVEMENT OF LEARNING OUTCOMES CONTAINING BLOOM'S SKILLS—EMPHASIS ON TRANSFERABILITY | | |
|---|---|---|
| APPLY MULTIPLE MEANS OF GETTING LEARNERS INTERESTED IN LEARNING (ENGAGEMENT) | | |
| PROVIDE MULTIPLE TYPES OF LEARNING RESOURCES (REPRESENTATION) | | |
| PROVIDE MULTIPLE WAYS FOR LEARNERS TO DEMONSTRATE LEARNING (ACTION & EXPRESSION) | | |
| Pre-time with teachers and peers | Time with teachers and peers | Post-time with teachers and peers |
| Self-directed study | Teacher/peer-supported study | Self-directed study |
| Primarily for content engagement | Recap of content and key learning points covered during self-directed study | Opportunities to revisit in-session learning |
| Development of lower-order cognitive skills through low-demand activities | Primarily for supporting higher-order cognitive skills development | Evaluation to test capability to apply higher-order cognitive skills through formative assessment reflecting learning outcomes |
| Opportunities for self-assessment (feedback) of lower-order cognitive skills reflecting learning outcomes | Explanation and/or demonstration of higher-order skills | Opportunities for self-assessment |
| Opportunity for reflection on progress | Active collaborative practice of higher-order skills (active learning with peers) reflecting learning outcomes | Opportunity to reflect on progress |

| ACHIEVEMENT OF LEARNING OUTCOMES CONTAINING BLOOM'S SKILLS—EMPHASIS ON TRANSFERABILITY | | |
|---|---|---|
| APPLY MULTIPLE MEANS OF GETTING LEARNERS INTERESTED IN LEARNING (ENGAGEMENT) | | |
| PROVIDE MULTIPLE TYPES OF LEARNING RESOURCES (REPRESENTATION) | | |
| PROVIDE MULTIPLE WAYS FOR LEARNERS TO DEMONSTRATE LEARNING (ACTION & EXPRESSION) | | |
| Pre-time with teachers and peers | Time with teachers and peers | Post-time with teachers and peers |
| Opportunity for learners to ask questions, seek clarification, and give feedback | E-tivities reflecting learning outcomes | Opportunities for learners to ask questions, seek clarification, and give feedback |
| | Feedback-corrected practice (mastery-oriented feedback) | |
| | Active practice of higher-order skills should be repeated in this phase | |
| | Opportunity to reflect on progress | |
| | Opportunity for learners to ask questions, seek clarification, and give feedback | |

The Cheese Sandwich is a learner-centered approach that reflects UDL practices in the general sense, but with several important aspects emphasized. For example, it accounts for individual variation among learners, supports the varying of learning demands and optimization of challenges, helps to minimize threats and distractions, and supports the provision of mastery-oriented feedback, supporting learners to be "strategic and goal-directed" (CAST, 2018). The issue of mastery-oriented feedback is an important one, because it makes learner metacognition a more intentional and transparent part of how instructional experiences are designed and delivered for both learners and teachers. Teachers are not only supporting learner mastery of content but also supporting learners to figure out how they personally master content in their own way. Mastery-oriented feedback is covered in more detail in Chapter 12.

The ways in which the Cheese Sandwich supports engagement, representation, and action and expression are detailed in Tables 7-4 through 7-6.

**TABLE 7-4.** How the Cheese Sandwich Supports Engagement

| Preventing disengagement | • The flipped element of the Cheese Sandwich means that the time learners spend with their teachers and their peers is active and interactive as opposed to didactic and passive. The use of varied learning activities that reflect each learning outcome supports the *chunking* of learning, or dividing learning into digestible segments.<br>• The active learning activities that happen during the cheese part of the Cheese Sandwich require learners to think about what they're doing and practice the cognitive skills articulated in the learning outcomes. Learners are given opportunities to reflect on their progress with developing various cognitive skills, and identify their strengths and areas for development. |
|---|---|
| Preventing disinterest | • The first slice of bread in the Cheese Sandwich, which involves self-directed study, enables learners to give feedback on the learning experience before they've even met with their teachers and peers. Learners have the opportunity to provide feedback on what they'd like to learn and how they'd like to learn it at each stage of the Cheese Sandwich.<br>• At each part of the Cheese Sandwich, learners are able to provide feedback and speak candidly about their thoughts, feelings, and attitudes toward learning, the topic being studied, as well as their challenges and motivations for learning.<br>• Bloom's skills are inherent within the learning outcomes that span the entire Cheese Sandwich. Learners are made explicitly aware that Bloom's skills are transferable and can be transferred to different contexts beyond the topic of study, supporting lifelong learning and employment. |
| Preventing information overload | • In the Cheese Sandwich, learning is built around learning outcomes—the essential things that learners are required to know or do. Outcome-driven instruction helps to avoid "stuffing" learning experiences with content, ensuring that learning is lean and targeted.<br>• The feedback-corrected practice approach, which is a big part of the Cheese Sandwich, enables learners to check and correct their progress toward achieving learning outcomes. Feedback identifies strengths and the reasons for them (medals) as well as areas and guidelines for development (missions) to enable learners to target specific areas of their learning for improvement. Medals and missions are discussed in depth in Chapters 10 and 12. |

**TABLE 7-5.** How the Cheese Sandwich Supports Representation

| Avoiding text overload | • Most learning materials and resources in higher education have traditionally been text based, such as books and journals, which learners have largely been required to engage with during self-directed study to help them make sense of their learning. The Cheese Sandwich repurposes self-directed study by flipping the classroom, meaning that the "making sense" part of learning involves actively participating in active, collaborative learning activities. Hence, learners are not required to read lots of material to make sense of their learning.<br>• Through the flipped element of the Cheese Sandwich, content engagement happens during self-directed study, with content provided in a variety of ways, including several prerecorded multimedia options such as videos, screencasts, and podcasts. Learners can access multimedia content both before and after taught sessions, and it is available to them to access on their own devices too. |
|---|---|
| Preventing access issues | • All prerecorded multimedia content is made available to all learners and can be accessed at all times as part of self-directed learning.<br>• All learning covered when learners and teachers are together in class is available to review, replay, or revisit through various mechanisms including video recordings of didactic elements, notes, summaries, photos, tables, figures, graphic organizers, and the like.<br>• All learning materials, including handouts, activity instructions, links to websites, background information, and briefs for evaluation/assessment, are shared with all learners. |
| Activating background knowledge | • Learning glossaries are provided alongside prerecorded multimedia content to support familiarity with and subsequent learning of new and unfamiliar terms.<br>• At the start of the cheese part of the Cheese Sandwich, key learning points are recapped from the multimedia content accessed during self-directed study.<br>• During the cheese part of the Cheese Sandwich, learners are required to actively engage in active, collaborative learning activities that reflect the learning outcomes. Thus, they are required to apply cognitive skills to the content delivered ahead of sessions. |

TABLE 7-6. How the Cheese Sandwich Supports Action & Expression

| Capturing important information | • Through the clear commitment to enabling learners to review, replay, and revisit learning through various mechanisms (videos, notes, summaries, photos, tables, figures, graphic organizers, etc.), there is much less requirement for them to take notes during learning experiences. |
|---|---|
| Making contributions | • Learners have regular opportunities to ask questions anonymously through online chat options housed in the learning management system (LMS). When together with teachers and peers, they can make anonymous responses through various applications that allow collaboration, content sharing, questions, and so on (whether in physical or virtual sessions).<br>• During the cheese part of the Cheese Sandwich, learners are presented with a variety of active collaborative learning and evaluation activities that allow them to express themselves in different ways. Activities may involve discussion, questioning, problem solving, defending or challenging a position, implementing a strategy, or more.<br>• Learners are encouraged throughout the Cheese Sandwich to self-evaluate and self-reflect on their learning of whatever topic is studied. |
| Maintaining focus | • Prerecorded self-directed learning materials are limited to 20 minutes, duration and include built-in activities and knowledge checks to avoid loss of focus.<br>• When learners are together with teachers and peers, didactic elements are minimized, being limited to recapping important content.<br>• A variety of active collaborative learning and evaluation activities are utilized, with opportunities for learners to self-reflect, self-evaluate, and evaluate and give feedback to peers to avoid loss of focus. |

# EVIDENCE INFORMED

In his groundbreaking work *Visible Learning*, Professor John Hattie compared effect sizes of 259 different factors that influence learning outcomes as part of a large meta-analysis of more than 800 separate studies on learning and teaching (Hattie, 2012). An *effect size* is the quantitative measure of the size of the experimental effect between two variables. The larger the effect size, the stronger the relationship between the two variables. Hattie's work has enabled us to identify which factors have the largest effect on learning and attainment, including various learning and teaching methods and approaches.

Hattie established that the average effect size for all of the factors he examined was 0.4, a value he defines as the *hinge point*, which is basically a threshold. Any factors with an effect size larger than 0.4 are considered better than average, representing desirable factors and approaches related to learning and attainment. Indeed, Hattie uses a *barometer of influence* to sort the factors from those that have negative effects to those that have desired effects (Hattie, 2012).

The specific learning and teaching factors that have the greatest effect on learning and attainment are too numerous to mention here, but one clear observation is that many, like the Cheese Sandwich, are grounded in the cognitivist and constructivist schools of learning, requiring learners to undertake challenging active learning tasks involving the use of higher-order thinking skills to make meaning and solve problems. Feedback on learning was also found to be extremely important.

Another important observation is how many of the most influential factors essentially reflect a UDL approach to learning, teaching, and assessment. For example, many of the strategies above the hinge point refer to the importance of setting challenging learning goals and supporting and developing learner motivation, which closely aligns to the engagement principle of UDL. Many of the strategies above the hinge point also refer to different means of representing information related to learning—such as using vocabulary supports, mnemonics, concept maps, and organizers—and so closely reflect the representation principle of UDL. Other approaches with a large effect size, such as formative assessment, practice assessment, and the development of communication skills and strategies, reflect the action and expression principle of UDL. Strategies that intentionally require the use of higher-order thinking skills, such as cognitive task analysis, problem solving, and inductive tasks, rate high in terms of attainment, and the impact of metacognition on learning and attainment is a recurring theme. Therefore, a UDL approach to learning, teaching, and assessment aligns very closely with the most impactful approaches to supporting learning and attainment.

## TRANSFERABILITY

In Chapter 4, the Surface, Deep, and Transfer (Hattie et al., 2016) learning model was briefly mentioned in relation to the importance of developing transferable skills, particularly cognitive skills. The way in which learning is supported as part of the

Cheese Sandwich shares some similarities with this model. Briefly, the model focuses on how we can get learners from surface-level learning to a deeper level and then ultimately able to transfer their learning. Learning transfer is essentially using what we have learned in one context or scenario, including knowledge and skills, and transferring it to another one (Hattie et al., 2016).

The Cheese Sandwich espouses setting tasks that climb Bloom's taxonomy like a ladder (Petty, 2014), incorporating lower-order cognitive tasks that support surface- or rote-level learning before moving on to higher-order cognitive tasks to support deep or meaningful learning (Meyer, 2002). The aspects of the Cheese Sandwich that support metacognition through mastery-oriented feedback, self-assessment, and reflection support learners to develop strategies to learn and apply cognitive skills, particularly higher-order ones. The processes that learners develop for applying those skills can then be transferred to different contexts, as per the Transfer element of the model. As discussed in Chapter 4, there's an ever-increasing focus on lifelong learning, transferability of skills, and employability in higher education, with learners required to develop transferable skills in addition to content or subject knowledge. Frequently, it is cognitive skills, rather than content, that can be directly transferred and applied to different contexts. During the Cheese Sandwich process, learners are made explicitly aware that Bloom's skills are transferable to different contexts beyond the topic of study, supporting lifelong learning and employment. With its emphasis on cognitive skills development, the Cheese Sandwich supports the modern need for transferability, making it well aligned for the needs of modern students.

This is not to suggest that the Cheese Sandwich approach is a learning and teaching panacea. There may be situations and scenarios that do not lend themselves to this instructional design approach for a variety of reasons, including the nature of the subject to be taught, time and scheduling requirements, and other professional or regulatory requirements. This book is not a plea for you to abandon your current approach in favor of the Cheese Sandwich, especially if your current approach is more appropriate to your circumstances; instead, it's a means of encouraging you to reflect on your current approach to instructional design, think about learner variability, and consider how you're catering to learner needs through the removal or reduction of barriers. It's also a means of encouraging you to adopt and apply sound pedagogic principles and approaches to support learning, particularly those approaches that are known to positively impact learning.

Although it may not work for everyone, the Cheese Sandwich is a means of intelligently designing important learning and teaching elements into the instructional experience, such as the parts of the Roadmap for Teaching. Including each part of the roadmap in an instructional experience is difficult in scenarios where the teacher's main role is to deliver content, which, as you now know, is typically what higher education teachers do. The Cheese Sandwich is also a clear way to support learners with aspects of their learning that they typically find difficult, such as understanding and applying higher-order cognitive skills through increased teacher and peer support and increased feedback. What makes higher education "higher" is engagement with those higher-order skills that enable learners to think critically, solve problems, and develop their ideas, and the Cheese Sandwich lends itself well to this endeavor. So, even if you don't replace your current instructional design approach with the Cheese Sandwich, you can at least utilize elements of it to enhance your current teaching practice. My main hope is that the Cheese Sandwich has at least got you thinking about learning design.

# 8

## The Cheese Sandwich and How People Learn

According to Phil Race (2019), teaching is about facilitating learning, or "making learning happen" among learners. Race argues that making learning happen is about providing and supporting the conditions that underpin how people learn. Based on several decades of evidence-based inquiry into how learners learn, Race (2019) proposed a model based on seven critical factors:

1. Wanting to learn
2. Needing to learn
3. Learning by doing
4. Feedback
5. Making sense
6. Verbalizing
7. Assessing

The model came to be known as "ripples on a pond" because of how these critical factors for learning are said to interact with each other; specifically, they don't play out linearly or as part of a cycle, but they all affect each other. Unlike ripples on an actual pond, the "ripple" here doesn't have to begin in the same place (the center) each time, emanating outward. In this model, the ripples from one factor can move in various directions to affect other factors. For example, learning may begin with *wanting* or *needing* to learn something, which in turn may be continually influenced by a ripple from *feedback*. *Learning by doing* may also be influenced by a ripple from *feedback*, which may itself influence *making sense*, and so on. There are numerous possible interactions between different factors.

Regardless of the relationships between the factors, each one must be present as part of the learning experience if effective learning is to take place. Fortunately, the Cheese Sandwich and associated Roadmap for Teaching provide opportunities for learners to experience all of the seven factors.

## WANTING TO LEARN

The UDL principle of engagement, which runs through the Cheese Sandwich (Table 7-1), reflects the need to provide multiple ways of getting learners interested in their learning and supporting their continued commitment and motivation. For example, the engagement principle in the UDL Guidelines includes specific sections on recruiting interest, sustaining effort and persistence, and self-regulating emotions and motivation (CAST, 2018). Hence, application of the engagement principle of UDL strongly supports the factor of *wanting* to learn.

## NEEDING TO LEARN

In situations when the desire to learn is low, it is important to support *needing* to learn as a means of sustaining interest, persistence, and commitment to learning. To enhance the "needing to learn" factor, you can use clear learning goals or outcomes and emphasize their importance and relevance to learners. In alignment with checkpoint 8.1 in the CAST UDL Guidelines (2018), which states that teachers should "heighten the salience of goals and objectives," the Cheese Sandwich emphasizes learning goals or outcomes and the transferability of the cognitive skills they contain.

The constructive alignment approach (Biggs & Tang, 2011) inherent within the Cheese Sandwich—that is, the clear alignment between learning goals or outcomes, learning activities, and assessment tasks—further heightens the salience of goals and objectives by critically linking teaching to assessment. As the saying goes, "learning is driven by assessment," and thus linking learning goals directly to assessment can enhance the need to learn.

## LEARNING BY DOING

The Cheese Sandwich espouses the importance of learning actively, or learning by doing. Specifically, the cheese in the Cheese Sandwich, during which learners develop higher-order thinking skills with the support of teachers and peers, is underpinned by learning by doing. As mentioned in Chapter 7, the Cheese Sandwich emphasizes learning and teaching approaches above John Hattie's hinge point (Hattie, 2012), which generally require learners to undertake challenging active learning tasks. Learning actively rather than passively supports the active practice of higher-order thinking skills, providing an outlet for feedback-corrected practice and eventual mastery of higher-order skills.

## FEEDBACK

As you've learned, the Cheese Sandwich is the vehicle for implementing the Roadmap for Teaching. A critical feature of the Roadmap for Teaching is *feedback*, which is applied formatively at two critical points: 1) when the learners are engaging in learning activities, and 2) following completion of evaluation activities. In the Cheese Sandwich, not only do learners receive feedback from their teachers as they engage in learning and evaluation activities, but they also have the opportunity to give and receive it from their peers, since peer collaboration and support are core characteristics of the Cheese Sandwich.

## MAKING SENSE

*Making sense* refers to the process learners go through to "digest" their learning. It is about how they reach the point where they "get it" (Race, 2019). Race (2019) suggests that in learning situations, learners are literally surrounded by people who can support them with the making sense stage. Since the Cheese Sandwich emphasizes how to make best use of the time learners spend with teachers and peers, the *making sense* factor is an inherent feature of its design. As above, peer collaboration and support are core characteristics of the Cheese Sandwich.

## VERBALIZING

*Verbalizing* is about learners putting their learning into spoken words to other people (Race, 2019). Indeed, Race (2019) posits that verbalizing learning is an important aspect of the *making sense* part of learning. As above, the focus on peer-to-peer learning and support within the Cheese Sandwich means that learners have significant opportunities to verbalize their learning with their peers. In addition to supporting the making sense aspect, verbalizing is learning by doing and provides an outlet for feedback. Furthermore, it can be an important type of evaluation activity within the Cheese Sandwich.

## ASSESSING

In the Cheese Sandwich model, learners have multiple opportunities to assess their own and their peers' learning through self-assessment tasks, peer-supported study, and various evaluation activities. According to Race (2019), being able to assess one's own work as well as that of others supports the ability to make critical judgments and/or apply criteria to evidence learning, which in turn deepens learning. As discussed earlier, evaluation activities that represent a clear and intentional part of the Cheese Sandwich provide opportunities for *assessing*.

> **PAUSE AND THINK** Review Phil Race's seven critical factors for learning. How many of them are part of the instructional experiences/teaching sessions you deliver? Which ones are missing? Is it possible for you to include them in your teaching?

# Part III

# Designing for Mastery

# 9
# Goal-Directed Learning

It is critically important to recognize that learning goals or outcomes are central to engagement, a core principle of UDL. The extensive meta-analysis of research studies on learning and attainment that forms the basis of John Hattie's excellent *Visible Learning* (Hattie, 2012) demonstrates that establishing challenging learning goals or outcomes is an effective means of setting learner expectations, as well as an essential prerequisite for meaningful and effective learning. Numerous scholars of learning and teaching have advised that setting difficult but achievable learning goals or outcomes supports learner engagement and intrinsic learner motivation.

The overall aims of UDL are to support the development of expert learners who are "purposeful and motivated," "resourceful and knowledgeable," and "strategic and goal-directed." In this chapter, we'll focus on the strategic and goal-directed aim of UDL.

As noted in Chapter 5, for learners to be strategic and goal directed, they need to have a goal or goals to aim for. In our role as teachers, we can support this process by ensuring that each of our teaching sessions is accompanied by a set of intended learning outcomes or goals. As mentioned in Chapter 2, the term *goals* is used interchangeably with the term *outcomes* to mean what learners must "know" or be able to "do" as a result of their learning. In the British context within which I work, it is commonplace to use the term *learning outcomes* when referring to *learning goals* from an instructional design perspective. Furthermore, since this part of the book is about applying the Roadmap for Teaching, in which learning outcomes are a critical component, I'll use *learning outcomes* or *outcomes* to refer to learning goals throughout.

So, what exactly is a learning outcome? Quite simply, it specifies to learners what they should have learned or be able to do by the end of a period of learning. Thus, learning outcomes are learner- rather than teacher-centered. Contrast this with aims and objectives, which were used instead of learning outcomes for many years in higher education as part of the design of teaching sessions, modules/units, and programs.

*Aims* are broad statements about the purpose of a particular unit or program of learning, and *objectives* are the steps required to achieve the aims in relation to how the teacher will structure and present the learning. Aims and objectives don't tell us much about what learners will learn or be able to do as a result of their learning, and thus are perhaps of more benefit to teachers than to learners. In other words, aims and objectives are largely teacher-centered, whereas outcomes are learner-centered and reflect a relatively recent movement from a teacher-focused approach to higher education to a more learner-focused one. Critically, learning outcomes provide learners with the goals toward which they can focus strategic learning actions. As I've noted previously, I like to think of learning outcomes as akin to the destination of a journey. If you don't have a clear destination in mind when you're on a journey, you won't know where you're going or how to get there. This is why learning outcomes are a critical part of backward design—once you know where you want to get to, you can work backward to create a pathway to get there.

## PROGRAM-LEVEL OUTCOMES

Programs of learning will have learning outcomes that generally provide information on what the learner is expected to be able to demonstrate by the time the program has been completed. The program's assessment processes (usually undertaken at the module or unit level) provide the mechanism for determining whether the learners have achieved the program-level learning outcomes.

## MODULE- OR UNIT-LEVEL OUTCOMES

Individual modules or units of study within a program also have learning outcomes, and these outcomes should reflect the program-level learning outcomes, since learners are generally assessed at the module or unit level rather than the program level. Hence, module learning outcomes, if written well, should directly reflect the module's assessments.

## SESSION-LEVEL OUTCOMES

Finally, individual teaching sessions should have learning outcomes that reflect the module or unit learning outcomes. If module learning outcomes reflect the module assessments (as they should), then the learning that happens during teaching sessions should support successful assessment outcomes for the corresponding modules or units. Therefore, *one of the main purposes for using session-level learning outcomes is to help align teaching with assessment*, and this is an inherent feature of the Cheese Sandwich as discussed in previous chapters.

As described in Chapter 7, the Cheese Sandwich represents a block of learning—that is, all of the learning and teaching activity that supports the learning of a given topic or content area, which will usually include individual teaching sessions, or times when learners, teachers, and peers are together in a physical or virtual space, in addition to self-directed study. Rather than those individual teaching sessions being the only part of the learning process with learning outcomes, as is typically the case in higher education, the entire block of learning specifies learning outcomes, meaning learners can be working toward the achievement of some learning outcomes during self-directed study.

To summarize, session-level learning outcomes, or learning outcomes that belong to a block of learning as per the Cheese Sandwich, should support the achievement of module-level learning outcomes, which in turn should support the achievement of program-level learning outcomes. As Figure 9-1 shows, there should be direct alignment between session/block-, module-, and program-level learning outcomes.

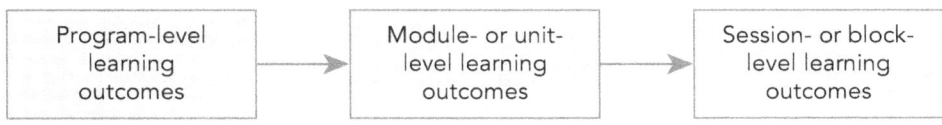

**FIGURE 9-1.** Alignment between program-, module-, and session-level learning outcomes

## WRITING LEARNING OUTCOMES

When writing learning outcomes, aim to describe what the learners will be expected to be able to do by the time the program, module or unit, or individual teaching session or block of learning (as per the Cheese Sandwich) is completed.

You should always also include a mechanism for measuring the extent to which the learners have achieved the outcomes. At the module or unit level, this is obvious; the summative assessments for the module or unit will reflect whether learners have met the learning outcomes. However, this aspect is less obvious in individual teaching sessions or Cheese Sandwich–style blocks of learning, which may well possess learning outcomes but not necessarily a way of measuring the extent to which the learners have achieved them. This is why, whether they are written at the program, module or unit, or session/block level, learning outcomes should always be accompanied by an evaluation mechanism. As covered in Chapter 7, the entire Cheese Sandwich includes learning outcomes aligned with the outcomes for the module/unit to which the specific Cheese Sandwich belongs.

Considering this context, it isn't useful to write a learning outcome in terms of what a learner will *understand* by the end of a period of learning, because it's very difficult to measure understanding due to the multiple ways in which it could be defined. For example, to *understand* a concept could be to merely *describe* it, or it could represent more complex cognitive processes such as to *critically evaluate* or *analyze* the concept. With *understanding* defined in such a vague way, measurement becomes very challenging.

It's of far greater value to frame the outcome in relation to how learners can *demonstrate* understanding so that checking can take place more effectively.

Let's take this example: "This session will help you to understand the anatomy of the heart."

This isn't a very good learning outcome; it would be very difficult to measure whether learners have actually achieved the required level of understanding.

A better example might be: "By the end of this session, you'll be able to label the major anatomical structures found in the human heart."

In this example, understanding is relatively straightforward to measure, since it would involve a simple task in which learners label the major anatomical structures of the heart.

When writing learning outcomes, keep the following tips in mind:

- **Use future tense.** Always use the future tense; for example, "By the end of this session/block of learning, you'll be able to . . . ."

- **Represent the most important information/content.** Ask yourself, "What do I want the learners to learn or be able to do by the end of the program/module/session/block of learning?" The answer will help you to identify the most important information the learners must learn so that you can base the learning outcomes on that content.

- **Make sure outcomes are clear and SMART.** Make sure the outcomes are clear and unambiguous. Can they realistically be achieved in the given timeframe, and are they measurable as part of a knowledge check or check for understanding? Keep your learners in mind when you write learning outcomes. It can be useful to use the acronym SMART: Specific, Measurable, Achievable, Realistic, and Timely.

- **Use straightforward language and avoid jargon.** A learner will have a much higher likelihood of achieving a learning outcome if they clearly understand what it means and what's being asked of them.

- **Include process outcomes as well as product outcomes.** Avoid the common pitfall of reflecting only the products of learning, such as the end product of the assessment process. For example, instead of having an outcome stating, "By the end of the module, you'll be able to write a laboratory report," say, "By the end of the module, you'll be able to devise, write, and implement a laboratory report." The second outcome is more useful because it provides clear information on the process the learners must go through to complete the assessment, not just the end product of the assessment process.

- **Pitch at the appropriate level.** Make sure outcomes are targeted to the appropriate level. See the section "Learning Outcome Levels" for more information.

- **Include multiple outcome types.** Balance different outcome types, including knowledge, application, and skills-based outcomes. See the next section, "Types of Learning Outcomes," for more information.

- **Separate learning outcomes from the means of achieving them.** Learning outcomes in higher education are often fixed and non-negotiable. However, the means of achieving learning outcomes can be entirely flexible. For example, an outcome might be to "Discuss the pros and cons of the UK leaving the European Union." Achieving this outcome could take many forms, such as an essay, verbal conversation, presentation, debate, or poster. There's rarely only one way to achieve an outcome.

## TYPES OF LEARNING OUTCOMES

To ensure that your learners develop a range of skills and learning experiences, it can be useful to include different types of outcomes when planning programs, modules or units, teaching sessions, and even Cheese Sandwich–style instructional experiences. There are three common learning outcome types:

**Knowledge-based outcomes**   These are the most common types of learning outcome. With knowledge-based outcomes, learners acquire a collection of defined content knowledge by the end of a program, unit, teaching session, or block of learning.

**Application-based outcomes**   These are practical skills that relate to the applied use of knowledge and refer to the way in which learners can engage critically with knowledge at higher levels of learning. This may include evaluating, analyzing, or synthesizing knowledge. In this respect, it can be useful to think of application-based outcomes as the application of Bloom's cognitive skills.

**Skills-based outcomes**   These are intellectual and transferable skills. Effective learning will include some skills development in addition to knowledge acquisition. At the module or unit level particularly, it can be useful to combine transferable skills-based learning outcomes—such as academic writing, information searching, and communication skills—with subject-specific skills.

## LEARNING OUTCOME LEVELS

It's important to ensure that you are writing learning outcomes at an appropriate level for the learning group. A common way of doing so is to use Bloom's taxonomy of educational objectives (Figure 9-2). As Chapter 4 explained, the taxonomy is essentially a hierarchy of cognitive skills, with the lower-order skills at the bottom and the higher-order ones at the top.

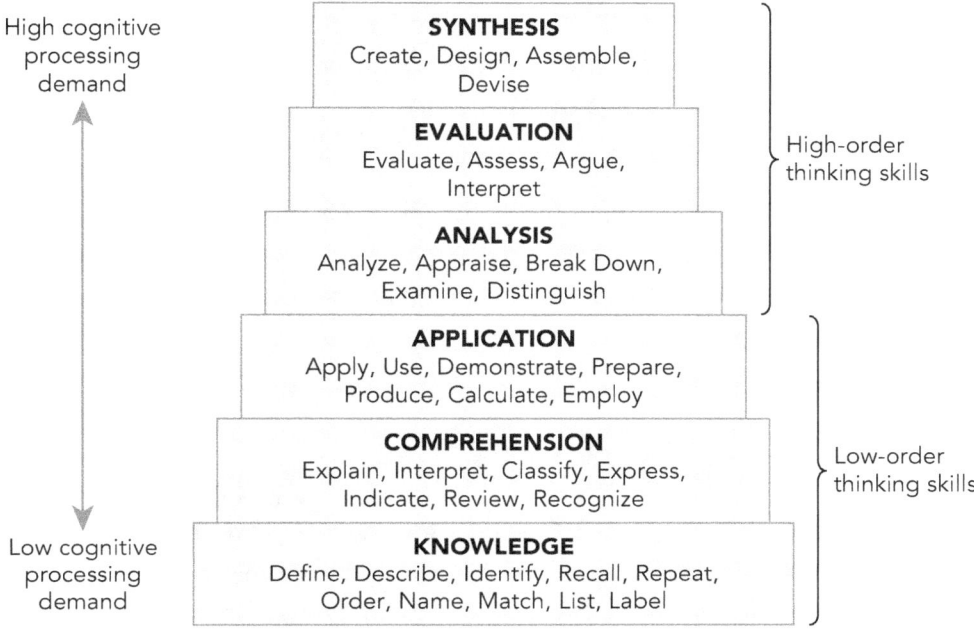

**FIGURE 9-2.** Bloom's taxonomy

Generally speaking, lower levels of learning, such as the first year of an undergraduate study program, will require learning outcomes mostly consisting of the lower-order skills, whereas higher levels of learning, when a learner reaches their final or senior year, will require outcomes consisting mostly of the higher-order skills. However, this isn't a hard-and-fast rule; lower levels can include higher-order skills and higher levels can include lower-order skills. Sometimes the nature of the subject being studied will determine this. For example, in anatomy and physiology, learners will still be required to describe, list, identify, and classify (all lower-order skills in Bloom's taxonomy) various anatomical and physiological structures, even at relatively senior levels of learning. In this case, though, the complexity of those lower-order skills will be higher. It's more challenging to identify the anatomical components that support respiration at the cellular level, for instance, than it is to identify gross anatomical structures such as various bones and muscles. However, the cognitive skill involved, identification, is the same.

Conversely, it's important to stretch and challenge learners by setting learning outcomes with higher-order skills at relatively lower levels of learning, such as during the first undergraduate year. For example, since the central aim of UDL is to support the development of expert learners (CAST, 2018), and the starting point for developing expertise when learning anything is to be able to master Bloom's skills, the earlier learners can begin practicing the higher-order skills during their learning journey, the more likely it is that they will achieve mastery over them. Remember, though, that learners won't be able to do the higher-order skills without first developing the lower-order skills. While it's possible to recall something without understanding it, it's not feasible to expect learners to use knowledge that they haven't first been able to recall.

**PAUSE AND THINK** Do you currently set learning outcomes for the instructional experiences/teaching sessions you design and deliver? Are they SMART? Do they include verbs from Bloom's taxonomy? Are they predominantly knowledge-, application-, or skills-based, or a mixture of all three? Do you need more of any particular outcome type? Do they align to module/unit learning outcomes?

# 10

## Learning Activities

As covered in Chapter 5, learning activities are what the learners *do* in order to learn the topic at hand. As before, note the emphasis on the word *do*, because it reiterates the critical point that learners must learn actively, not passively, especially when learning the higher-order thinking skills in Bloom's taxonomy. For example, to be able to *analyze*, or *evaluate*, learning content, learners must be given the opportunity to actively practice the skills. They won't be able to master such skills passively through some sort of osmosis!

## ALIGNMENT

Thinking back to the Roadmap for Teaching covered in Chapter 5, learning outcomes represent the goals of learning because they establish what the learner should be able to do with content once some learning has been completed. Subsequently, learning activities represent the means by which learners achieve their learning outcomes because they should require the learners to use content in the way the learning outcomes stipulate.

Recall the hypothetical learning outcome included in Chapter 5, "By the end of this class you'll be able to *distinguish* between the learning theories of constructivism and behaviorism." In this scenario, the learning activities should require the learners to actually do some *distinguishing* (the cognitive skills) between the theories of constructivism and behaviorism (the content). Of course, it's also critical for the learners to be able to tell us what they know about the content, which in this case is represented by the learning theories of constructivism and behaviorism. This aspect of learning—knowledge about topics, concepts, and facts—is sometimes called *declarative knowledge* (Biggs, 2003). However, for learners to learn deeply and really develop mastery over their learning, they must be able to show how they can use content—that is, apply knowledge during other tasks—which is sometimes known as *functioning knowledge* (Biggs, 2003). Put simply, the lower-order skills in Bloom's taxonomy are more reflective of declarative knowledge, with the higher-order skills collectively more reflective of functioning knowledge. As stated previously, the higher-order skills are more challenging to learn than the lower-order ones, and thus will require extensive practice if they are to be mastered and functional knowledge achieved. Learning activities provide an opportunity for learners to practice Bloom's skills. Without practice, they will not master Bloom's skills, particularly the higher-order ones.

## PRACTICE

Unfortunately, despite learning activities being opportunities for learners to practice the cognitive skills required for mastery, we sometimes see misalignment between learning outcomes and the learning activities used to achieve them. For example, a teacher may set a learning outcome stating that by the end of a block of learning their learners will be able to *create* or *solve*, two skills that represent functioning knowledge and are virtually impossible to master without practice. However, if the teacher then limits the learning activities to passively listening to the transmission of content in a lecture, then the opportunity to actually practice creating or solving will be missed. Transmitting content in this way might support the learners in knowing something about the content, but it is unlikely to help them use it in the way intended. It not only would negatively impact the learners' capability to *create* or *solve*, but also would be pretty boring, potentially diminishing their engagement (see the next section). Although hypothetical, this example highlights the criticality of ensuring that learning activities directly align to learning outcomes and require the learners to learn actively rather than passively if they are to develop functioning knowledge and master their learning.

# ENGAGEMENT

Learning activities are absolutely critical to the engagement principle of UDL, because they represent a huge and important part of a teacher's teaching methods. The methods a teacher uses when supporting learning perhaps have the largest influence on the application of the engagement principle, because they largely determine the level of interest, enjoyment, and value learners get from their learning. If you use a variety of fun, interesting, enjoyable, and authentic (that is, providing a realistic preview of the skills required for employment) learning activities in your teaching sessions, it's much more likely that your learners will want to come to class and participate in them. Thus, learning activities have a critical role to play in the recruiting interest aspects of engagement, because active participation in learning through active learning activities optimizes the relevance, value, and authenticity of learning, as stated in checkpoint 7.2 of the UDL Guidelines (CAST, 2018). Contrast this with the preceding example, where the primary learning activity is passively listening to the transmission of facts in a lecture. Would this get all of the learners interested in learning? It's no surprise that many learners fall asleep in the lecture hall. They're simply uninterested in the passive learning activity they are required to engage in, and as a result, many disengage totally.

As discussed in Chapter 2, engagement is essentially about attention and commitment. Commitment is related to the level of challenge a learner experiences when learning, and how learners are able to regulate those feelings of challenge—how they deal with those uncomfortable feelings of challenge as they "learn to learn" through metacognitive processes. A learner can't really be engaged if they're not challenged, so learning activities should be progressively challenging and scaffolded. As discussed in Chapter 9, setting challenging outcomes supports learner engagement and motivation. Since learning activities should directly reflect learning outcomes, it is self-evident that learning activities should also reflect the challenge encompassed in those learning outcomes. Challenge is essential to engagement, but it increases the probability of failure. However, with UDL we must reframe failure by making it a normal part of learning and something to be embraced. Feedback-corrected practice, discussed in Chapters 4 and 12, is essentially based on trial and error. Notice the word *error*: We make errors or mistakes as we practice cognitive skills. We then learn from those errors and try again until we master the skill. Coping with challenge is related to how well learners monitor their own progress, as Chapter 12 will discuss in more depth.

## VARIETY

As well as engaging learners more effectively, providing a variety of learning activities supports more effective learning among your learners. As you know, from a UDL perspective, learning outcomes should be separate from the means of achieving them. This means that there's no single type of learning activity that will enable all learners to achieve learning outcomes. Some learners will do better working individually on solving problems or attempting tasks, whereas others will benefit from working with their peers as part of group-based activities. Some learners will happily read a passage of text, highlighting and organizing key points, as opposed to others who might prefer more hands-on activities that require organizing and sorting information in a more visual and tangible form. The point here is that there should always be a variety of learning activities on offer, since different types of activities will engage a larger proportion of learners and support multiple pathways to achieve the learning outcomes. Part of becoming an expert learner, as per the key aim of UDL, is for the learner to get to know their own optimal means of achieving learning outcomes. They require our support in order to do this, and providing a variety of learning activities is a quick and easy way we can support them to this end. Please remember, though, that the variety of activities you offer will be driven by the variability of your learners and how that variability gives rise to barriers in the learning environment. It's not about mindlessly providing lots of different options just for the sake of it, but rather intentionally offering choices as a way to remove or reduce barriers. To be able to do this, you must first get to know your learners and understand the barriers they face, as covered in Chapter 3.

## FEEDBACK

Remember from Chapter 5's discussion of the Roadmap for Teaching that participation in learning activities provides an opportunity for feedback. Feedback about learners' attempts to use the cognitive skills articulated in learning outcomes, especially the higher-order ones, is absolutely essential, because it ensures that the learners are correctly interpreting and practicing the cognitive skills articulated in those learning outcomes. If learners are interpreting or practicing skills incorrectly, feedback will enable them to modify their practice accordingly. Of course, feedback is also essential to reinforce learning in circumstances where learners have interpreted and practiced the skills correctly.

When giving feedback on learner participation in learning activities, it is important to use what Geoff Petty calls "medals" and "missions." A feedback medal tells the learner what they did well when participating in a learning activity (Petty, 2014). Critically, the medal also provides some information on *why* they did the activity well. It is vital for learners to know why they've done something well because they might not be aware themselves. Conversely, a feedback mission tells the learner what they could improve upon when participating in learning activities (Petty, 2014). The mission also provides some information on *how* to improve because it's unlikely that the learner will know how to do so themselves. Providing information on why something was done well as part of a feedback medal, and on how to improve as part of a feedback mission, helps learners develop effective learning habits and practices that they can apply in the future, supporting their continued growth as effective, expert learners. Feedback medals and feedback missions are covered in more detail in Chapter 12.

Applying feedback in this way is part of feedback-corrected practice (Petty, 2014), which has been mentioned several times in the previous chapters and is covered in greater depth in Chapter 12. Essentially, learners should practice skills with feedback as part of a continuous loop until they have mastered them (Petty, 2014) as per checkpoint 8.4 in the UDL Guidelines: "increase mastery-oriented feedback" (CAST, 2018). Without feedback, it is unlikely that learners can master skills. Mastery-oriented feedback is covered in more detail in Chapter 12.

# EVALUATION

Although evaluation of learning will be covered in detail in Chapter 11, it's worth mentioning evaluation now in relation to learning activities. As discussed above, learning activities provide learners with the opportunity to practice the cognitive skills required for mastery. They can also practice practical skills through learning activities. Whether cognitive or practical, skills should be practiced continuously with feedback until they are mastered. Eventually, though, we must evaluate the application of those skills, which is why the Roadmap for Teaching (presented in Chapter 5) includes evaluation activities—that is, the way in which learners demonstrate their learning. Evaluation activities represent the natural next step after participation in learning activities. The purpose of a teaching session is that the learners learn something (perhaps we should call them "learning sessions" instead). The only real way for the teacher and the learner to know if the learners have truly learned anything is to somehow evaluate that learning. Evaluation activities also provide another important outlet for feedback. Thus, when planning teaching sessions, it is essential that you give evaluation activities as much consideration as the other elements of the Roadmap for Teaching—learning outcomes, learning activities, and opportunities for feedback.

# MASTERING SKILLS THROUGH PRACTICE

Learning activities enable learners to master various cognitive and practical skills through repeated, feedback-corrected practice. According to Petty (2014), learning activities satisfy an important learning need—to "use" or "practice" the skills being learned. Petty also notes that there are several other important needs that must be met as learners attempt to master skills by practicing them as part of learning activities. To remind us of the learning needs we must meet when supporting learners to master various skills, Petty helpfully put together the wonderful mnemonic *EDUCARE?*, which stands for *Explain, Doing detail, Use, Check and correct, Aide memoir, Review, Evaluate,* and *Questions* (see Table 10-1).

**TABLE 10-1.** The EDUCARE? Approach to Mastering Skills (Adapted From Petty, 2014)

| E | Explain | The skill being taught should be explained to the learners. What does it mean? Why is it important? Why do they need to learn it? |
|---|---|---|
| D | Demonstrate ("Doing detail" in the original) | Learners must be provided with a demonstration of the skill. It's important that they are shown how to do the skill before they attempt it for themselves. |
| U | Use | This is effectively practice. Learners must be given the opportunity to use or practice the skill through learning activities of their choosing. |
| C | Check and correct | Learner practice of the skill must be checked and corrected. This is where feedback with medals and missions is critical, and is part of the feedback-corrected practice loop discussed previously. |

| A | Aide memoir | Learners must be provided with a reminder or summary of the key points relating to the skill and its application. |
|---|---|---|
| R | Review | After learning a skill, learners must have the opportunity to review and reuse it consistently if they are to remain proficient in applying it. |
| E | Evaluate | Learners must be given the opportunity to demonstrate their learning to ensure that the skill has been learned correctly. |
| ? | Questions | Learners should have multiple opportunities to ask questions while learning the skill. |

Petty (2014) states that the Use and Check and correct elements are part of a cycle that repeats until skills are mastered, contributing to the feedback-corrected practice approach discussed earlier and represented in the Roadmap for Teaching. The cycle of feedback-corrected practice is shown in Figure 10-1.

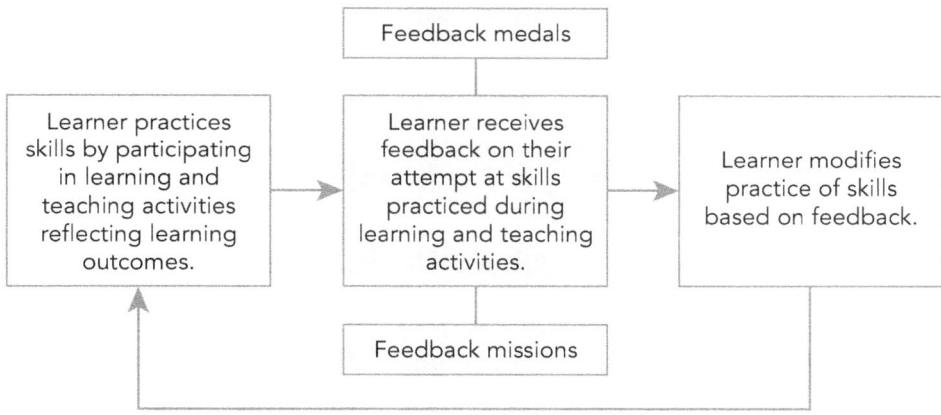

**FIGURE 10-1.** Feedback-corrected practice. Adapted from Petty (2014).

From a UDL perspective, it's important to remember that you can—indeed should—provide or facilitate each element of EDUCARE? through multiple means in line with the principles of UDL. For example, you could provide the Explain element using teacher talk, a prerecorded video, a downloadable handout, a podcast, a reading, or even a task or activity. To aid the learner's eventual mastery of a particular skill, you should explain it in different ways to support diverse approaches to and preferences for learning—and, of course, to remove barriers. The same goes for each element of EDUCARE?, as you can see in Table 10-2. The ideas in Table 10-2 are by no means exhaustive, so you're encouraged to think of as many inventive ways as possible to provide the elements of EDUCARE? with your own learners.

**TABLE 10-2.** Multiple Ways of Executing the EDUCARE? Elements (Adapted From Petty, 2014)

| E | Explain | Teacher talk, video, handout, reading, podcast, discovery task |
|---|---|---|
| D | Demonstrate ("Doing detail" in the original) | Teacher demonstration, video, podcast, peer demonstration |
| U | Use | A variety of activities encompassing the use of the skill that learners can choose; specific activities will depend on the skill being practiced |
| C | Check and correct | Teacher feedback, peer feedback, self-evaluation, self-check, and correct against an exemplar |
| A | Aide memoir | Summary, video, podcast, talking head, checklist |
| R | Review | A variety of activities encompassing the use of the skill that learners can choose; specific activities will depend on the skill being practiced |
| E | Evaluate | Assessment options that remove or reduce barriers to demonstrating understanding; specific outputs will depend on the skill being evaluated |
| ? | Questions | Hand up in class, online chat or forum, polling software, anonymous Post-it notes, email |

Getting learners to practice skills during learning activities and then providing feedback on them—as per the Use and Check and correct elements of EDUCARE?—is perhaps the most time-consuming activity that a teacher can administer during an instructional experience. As a result, many teachers feel that they simply don't have enough time to deliver content, set learning activities, repeat them with feedback, and then evaluate them as part of the instructional experiences they create. This is why the Cheese Sandwich approach, introduced in Chapter 7, is so critical to supporting mastery over learning. It repurposes the time learners spend with their teachers and peers to make time for practice, feedback, and subsequent mastery. Essentially, mastering cognitive or practical skills requires the presence of each element in the Roadmap for Teaching (Chapter 5) as part of the instructional experience. The Cheese Sandwich makes it possible to embed each roadmap element into instructional experiences because it focuses on supporting the development of functioning rather than declarative knowledge (Biggs, 2003). Learners can gain declarative knowledge during self-directed study, leaving them free to develop crucial functioning knowledge during time spent with teachers and peers.

**PAUSE AND THINK** What learning activities do you currently set for your learners? Do they align directly to the learning outcomes for your instructional experiences/teaching sessions? Do they provide the learners with an opportunity to practice important cognitive skills? Do learners receive feedback on their participation in learning activities?

# 11
## Demonstrating Understanding

In the broadest and most basic sense, learners demonstrate their understanding by completing summative assessments for the units or modules that they are studying. Units or modules will be underpinned by a set of intended learning outcomes. As covered in Chapter 9, learning outcomes are what the learners should have learned or be able to do by the conclusion of the unit or module. The assessment, of course, is the mechanism used to check that the learners have learned or can do whatever is specified in the learning outcomes. As such, it should directly reflect the intended learning outcomes for the units or modules it belongs to.

Learning outcomes will frequently be based on knowledge, application skills, or a combination of both. They will likely reflect the levels corresponding to the cognitive skills in Bloom's taxonomy, as discussed in Chapter 9. When assessments directly reflect the expected knowledge and skills found in the learning outcomes, we say they are *aligned*. For example, learning outcomes that use verbs such as *determine* and *evaluate* and an assessment that requires learners to *list* or *explain* wouldn't be aligned and thus wouldn't represent an appropriate or valid demonstration of understanding.

Another important step in the summative assessment process is the learning and teaching activities that happen in class on a session-by-session basis (covered in Chapter 10), as well as those that learners engage in during self-directed study. Learning and teaching activities provide learners with an opportunity to practice the skills articulated in the learning outcomes. Accordingly, they can play an important role in supporting summative assessment success, but only if they reflect the learning outcomes and subsequent assessments too. As per the example used in Chapter 10, we shouldn't expect summative assessment success when the assessment asks the learner to create or solve but the teaching has been confined to transmitting facts in lectures. Instead, the learners should have been given the opportunity to create or solve as part of the learning and teaching activities.

Ensuring that learning outcomes, learning and teaching activities, and assessments all line up, or ensuring *constructive alignment* (Biggs, 2003; Biggs & Tang, 2011), represents a critical part of supporting learners to become "strategic and goal-directed," as per the aims of UDL. Constructive alignment is also covered in Chapters 5 and 8.

As well as demonstrating understanding through summative assessment processes at the unit or module level, learners can also demonstrate understanding in a more formative way. Formative assessment is sometimes called assessment *for* learning, and it is generally intended to help teachers and learners monitor learning, providing ongoing feedback to help learners identify their strengths and areas for development. It typically involves qualitative feedback rather than grades, and it focuses on the aspects the learners did well, sometimes called the medal, and those that learners could improve upon, sometimes called the mission (Petty, 2014), as covered in Chapter 10. Formative assessment is also used as a source of information to provide differentiated instruction and feedback, as discussed in Chapter 5. When reflective of unit or module learning outcomes and assessments, formative assessment can be a powerful way of supporting learning and preparing learners for summative assessments because it helps them practice, evaluate, and receive feedback on the knowledge and skills they will be assessed on during the summative assessments.

Sometimes teachers express concern over setting formative assessments because they worry that learners won't bother to complete them if the assessments don't count toward final grades. One potential way around this problem is to incorporate formative assessments into the summative assessment process. A common way of doing so is to use a *patchwork-style assessment* (Winter, 2003), which requires the learners to complete a piece, or *patch*, of formative assessment at regular intervals, sometimes every week. The patches are not marked, but learners are given feedback on them. Usually each patch is linked to the summative assessment in some way by reflecting the tasks that encompass the summative assessment. The idea is that over the course of a unit or module, the learner completes the summative assessment but in formative fashion by completing the patches and receiving feedback on what they did well and areas for improvement. The learner will still have to create and submit a separate summative piece of work, but they'll have essentially done the work already by completing the patches regularly. They'll also have benefited from the ongoing feedback they received on each patch and so should be able to submit their best attempt at the summative stage. In some cases, learners are required to submit each patch in ongoing fashion, with submission being a requirement of the summative assessment process. The patches won't be marked, but the learner can't pass the summative aspect unless they've submitted all the patches. Some portfolio-based assessments work in a similar manner. Patchwork-style assessments may not be suitable for all assessment scenarios, but they can be effective for providing ongoing support and feedback to learners in a formative way that supports their success in summative assessment.

As discussed in Chapter 9, there should be alignment between program learning outcomes; module learning outcomes; and learning outcomes for individual teaching sessions or blocks of learning, which, as per Cheese Sandwich–type approaches (see Chapter 7), should reflect the module or unit learning outcomes. Because module learning outcomes reflect the module assessments, the learning that happens as part of instructional experiences should support successful assessment outcomes for the modules or units they are part of. Therefore, one of the main purposes for using learning outcomes is to help align teaching with assessment, as discussed in Chapter 9.

So, how do we get learners to demonstrate their understanding during instructional experiences such as individual teaching sessions or Cheese Sandwich–style blocks of learning? The process is very similar to the one we explored earlier for units or modules. Let's refer back to the Roadmap for Teaching, a simplified version of which is shown in Figure 11-1.

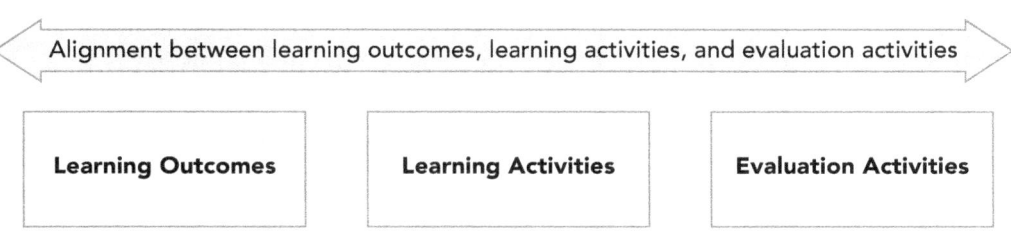

**FIGURE 11-1.** Simplified Roadmap for Teaching

The key elements required for teaching include intended learning outcomes, which, as you know, include information on what the learner should be able to do or know by the end of the learning experience. There should also be a mechanism for checking that the learners understand whatever it is they need to know or do. To revisit the example used in Chapter 10 about units and modules, the learning and teaching activities used within the instructional experience should reflect the learning outcomes and provide the learners with an opportunity to practice the skills articulated in those outcomes. Thus, if the outcomes state that learners will be able to *create* or *solve* following some learning, then the learning activities must involve them doing some creating and solving. The final step is to evaluate that the learners can create or solve using an evaluation activity that requires them to apply those skills. The specific evaluation task that learners undertake will depend upon the context within which the skills are being applied. However, it must require them to demonstrate the skills that they are required to learn as stipulated in the learning outcomes.

Applying the roadmap may seem like quite a daunting process. In traditional teaching scenarios, which may involve giving a lecture that lasts an hour, for example, there's a lot for the teacher to cover in a limited timeframe. Content delivery must sit alongside learning activities, evaluation activities, and the application of feedback. It's hard to do all of this in a one-hour session designed to transmit content. One way of overcoming the challenges of time constraints and trying to fit everything in is to utilize the Cheese Sandwich introduced in Chapter 7. With this approach, the time dedicated to achieving learning outcomes is repurposed, allowing a clear framework for learners to partly work toward their achievement during self-directed study time. Essentially, the Cheese Sandwich represents a block of learning where the time that learners spend with their teachers and peers is used to engage in learning activities that support mastery over skills via feedback-corrected practice. Conversely, self-directed learning that happens between times that learners spend with their teachers and peers is largely used for content engagement, evaluation of learning, and recap of learning. The main idea is that the Cheese Sandwich allows for including each element of the Roadmap for Teaching into the instructional experience, which, as stated, can be difficult to do in more traditional teaching scenarios such as lectures. See Chapter 7 for further details on the Cheese Sandwich.

**PAUSE AND THINK** Do you currently include evaluation activities as part of the design and delivery of the instructional experiences/teaching sessions you deliver? Do they align directly with the learning outcomes?

## ASSESSMENT

This is not a book about assessment, at least not summative assessment. I'm not a big fan of the word *assessment*. I feel it encourages too many teachers to focus solely on the products of learning, specifically emphasizing the high-stakes summative aspects of assessment for which learners are accountable, and ignoring the role assessment plays in both the learning process and the process of developing effective long-term study skills, habits, and strategies. Assessment is about so much more than gaining a sense of whether a learner has learned or not; however, such a discussion is beyond the scope of this book, which is principally concerned with instructional design and delivery from a "how to teach" perspective.

Despite my dislike of the word, when we evaluate whether learners have achieved learning outcomes during instructional experiences, we are effectively *assessing* their learning. However, I much prefer to use the word *evaluation* when referring to assessment in the instructional design context, since it sounds a little less harsh and is distinct from what we mean by summative assessment. It also lends itself much better to the evaluation activities described in the Roadmap for Teaching. Nonetheless, because *assessment* is the term commonly used in discussions of nonsummative evaluations of learning, such as formative assessment, I'll use that term when explaining the following ideas and concepts.

## ASSESSMENT *OF,* *FOR,* AND *AS* LEARNING

In my experience, assessing learning within the UDL framework is the area that teachers often find the most challenging. The difficulty often arises in the need to ensure that assessment is valid, fair, and equitable, but at the same time flexible and customizable. Common questions from teachers include the following:

- "If my learners are being assessed in different ways, how can I possibly assess them accurately?"

- "How do marking, feedback, and more importantly, grading, work if learners are demonstrating learning in different ways?"
- "How easy is it to compare different types of assessment?"
- "Surely it is unfair to compare different types of assessment?"

First, note that these are all valid concerns. In terms of the answers, we must think about how we can shift the emphasis from assessing the products of learning to assessing the progress learners make toward, and their attainment of, the learning outcomes. When contemplating a UDL assessment approach, it can be useful to split assessment into three forms: assessment *of* learning, assessment *for* learning, and assessment *as* learning.

## Assessment *of* Learning

Assessment *of* learning is essentially the same as summative assessment—that is, the extent to which a learner is able to make sense of the ideas, concepts, and skills found within and developed during a unit, module, or course of study. Summative assessments in this context represent the "performance tasks" that demonstrate whether learners have achieved the learning outcomes for the unit, module, or course in question, usually at the end of a period of instruction in high-stakes fashion involving grading (Earl & Katz, 2006; Kibble, 2017). Some important considerations for planning assessment of learning include flexibility, variety, the use of exemplars, the use of marking descriptors, *feed forward* (feedback in reverse, or what the learner should do in the future), and both product and process as inherent within the assessment and feedback process. Also, medals and missions, described briefly in Chapter 10 and more extensively in Chapter 12, are exceptionally important when feedback is given on summative work. As mentioned, this is a book about instructional design and delivery, and thus the completion of summative assessment is perhaps unlikely to directly figure into the instructional experience unless in particular circumstances where learners are required to complete ongoing pieces of work. An example would be the patchwork-style assessment discussed earlier in this chapter. However, even then, the patches that form part of the instructional experience are formative, not summative, with the summative piece completed separately from the instructional experience, as is often the case with many summative assessments. That said, the learning that learners engage in during the instructional experience will ultimately be directed toward and support the completion of summative assessments for the unit to which those experiences belong. Hence, instructional experiences, despite rarely involving any direct summative assessment, should be designed with summative assessment in mind.

## Assessment *for* Learning

Assessment *for* learning is formative assessment. It is intended to help teachers and learners monitor learning by gathering evidence that informs where the learners are in relation to their learning, the direction they need to take to achieve learning goals, and how they can be supported to achieve them (Gardner, 2011). Assessment for learning is used to provide ongoing feedback and help learners identify their strengths and areas for development. It is typically associated with qualitative feedback, dialogue, and feed forward rather than grades, and it focuses on what learners did well (the medal) and what they could improve upon (the mission). Formative assessment can be a powerful way of supporting learning and preparing learners for summative assessments because it helps them practice, evaluate, and receive feedback on the skills they will be assessed on during their summative assessments. It's important that formative assessments are varied, include medals and missions in feedback, and give learners the opportunity to assess both themselves and their peers.

**PAUSE AND THINK** Do you currently use assessment for learning (formative assessment) strategies as part of your instructional experiences/teaching sessions? If not, can you find a way to include assessment for learning?

Formative assessment is also a source of information upon which differentiated instruction and feedback can be based, as discussed in Chapter 7. Unlike assessment of learning, assessment for learning should be a clear and direct part of the instructional experience. Learners need to know how they are progressing, where their strengths lie, and what areas of their learning they need to improve upon. Similarly—and an area where assessment for learning is critical—teachers need to know how to modify their teaching as well as differentiate instruction and feedback. Assessment for learning is a key factor in supporting learners to achieve the two accomplishments associated with being an expert learner: 1) mastery over learning content, and 2) knowing how to personally master learning content. Thus, it is vital that you include assessment for learning as part of the design and delivery of your instructional experiences. The Cheese Sandwich, discussed in Chapter 7, shows how assessment for learning can be embedded into instructional experiences.

## Assessment *as* Learning

Assessment *as* learning is primarily designed to monitor progress and largely consists of self-assessment—supporting learners to develop an awareness of their personal learning strategies and habits. It is associated with self-regulation, self-monitoring, metacognition, and feedback (Evans, 2013; Lysaght & O'Leary, 2013; Sadler, 2010). With teacher support, learners can develop their capability to self-assess as a means of recognizing the approaches and strategies that support their learning most effectively. Assessment as learning can support strategy development and help learners to practice the skills they need to become more effective learners.

Essentially, assessment as learning is about them recognizing how they learn most effectively. This process involves supporting and encouraging learners to understand their personal motivations for learning, since such an awareness can help them develop the confidence to take risks when learning, as well as to stretch, grow, and develop the enthusiasm and independence required for effective higher education study.

A key function of assessment as learning is to help learners better understand how they're progressing as independent learners, which is a critical capability for studying in higher education. When learners can identify the areas they need to develop as learners, they are better equipped to comprehend the support and development they need, and proactively pursue the tools and assistance they require to support their achievement of learning outcomes. Typical examples of assessment as learning may include learners engaging in self-review and peer review of their work (Sadler, 2009) or using exemplars to assess their own and others' work (Carless, Salter, Yang, & Lam, 2011).

As with assessment for learning, assessment as learning is vital in supporting learners to become expert learners, particularly the metacognitive part—that is, knowing how to personally achieve mastery over learning content. If learners can't self-assess through assessment as learning, then they can't improve their learning. Hence, it's particularly important to include this piece in the design and delivery of your instructional experiences. Assessment as learning strategies should be aligned to learning outcomes.

**PAUSE AND THINK** Do you currently include opportunities for learners to self-assess and assess each other? How do your learners know what their learning strengths and areas for development are?

# 12

## The Criticality of Feedback

According to Sadler (1989), *feedback* is information provided to learners that is intended to reduce the gap between current and desired performance on a learning outcome. In this sense, the key purpose of feedback is to support learners to adjust their responses, which may involve their thinking and behaviors, to produce improved results against learning outcomes (Shute, 2008).

As discussed in Chapter 5, feedback is a core component of an ideal instructional experience and a key element of the Roadmap for Teaching (see Figure 12-1).

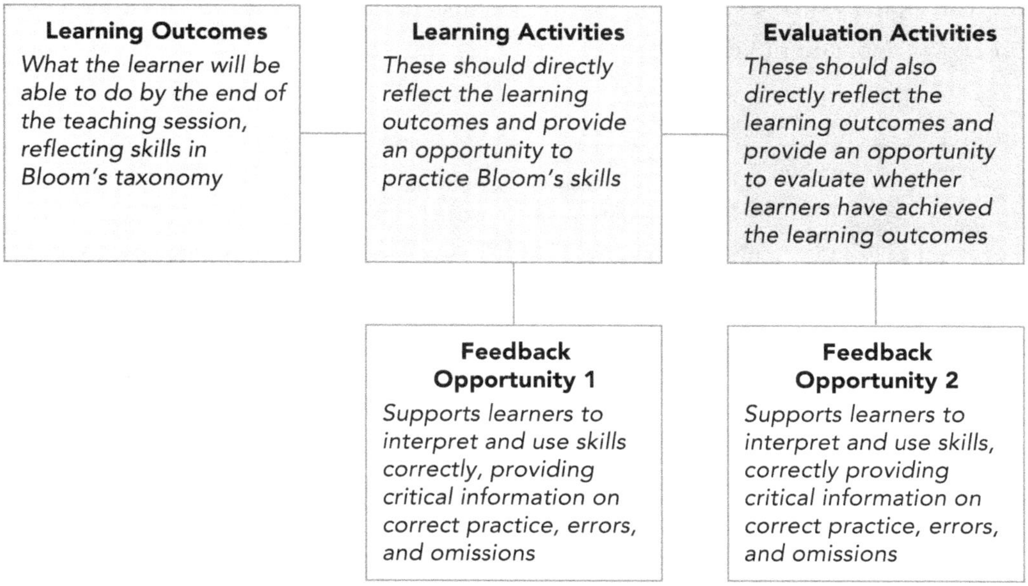

**Learning Outcomes**
*What the learner will be able to do by the end of the teaching session, reflecting skills in Bloom's taxonomy*

**Learning Activities**
*These should directly reflect the learning outcomes and provide an opportunity to practice Bloom's skills*

**Evaluation Activities**
*These should also directly reflect the learning outcomes and provide an opportunity to evaluate whether learners have achieved the learning outcomes*

**Feedback Opportunity 1**
*Supports learners to interpret and use skills correctly, providing critical information on correct practice, errors, and omissions*

**Feedback Opportunity 2**
*Supports learners to interpret and use skills, correctly providing critical information on correct practice, errors, and omissions*

**FIGURE 12-1.** The Roadmap for Teaching

Feedback is generated whenever learners are required to respond to a learning stimulus, which in the case of the Roadmap for Teaching occurs whenever learners engage in learning activities and attempt practice at various skills, and of course when those skills are evaluated as part of an evaluation activity. Although most common definitions of feedback describe it as a key mechanism for improving learner performance, it's equally critical for teachers to gain information on the effectiveness of their teaching methods and make adjustments accordingly (Hattie & Gan, 2011).

Several decades of research have demonstrated that feedback is one of the most important aspects of the learning experience, supporting successful learning and achievement (Hattie, 2012) as well as learner motivation and continued effort toward learning outcomes (Espasa & Meneses, 2010), which strongly reflects the engagement principle of UDL. Without feedback, learning will not happen effectively.

As discussed in Chapter 4, we construct our understanding of any given topic or concept based on what we already know about it. Unfortunately, when we construct understanding for ourselves, we can sometimes get it wrong and so our understanding requires some modification. Feedback is the driver for that modification of understanding. If feedback is missing or deficient, then modifying our understanding cannot happen appropriately and understandings are incomplete. Providing feedback on a learner's constructions of understanding, especially in an effort to help them correct that understanding, is one of the central reasons why teachers are so critical in supporting learning. Teachers are also critical for reinforcing understanding through feedback when the learner's construction *is* accurate. This feedback process is depicted in Figure 12-2.

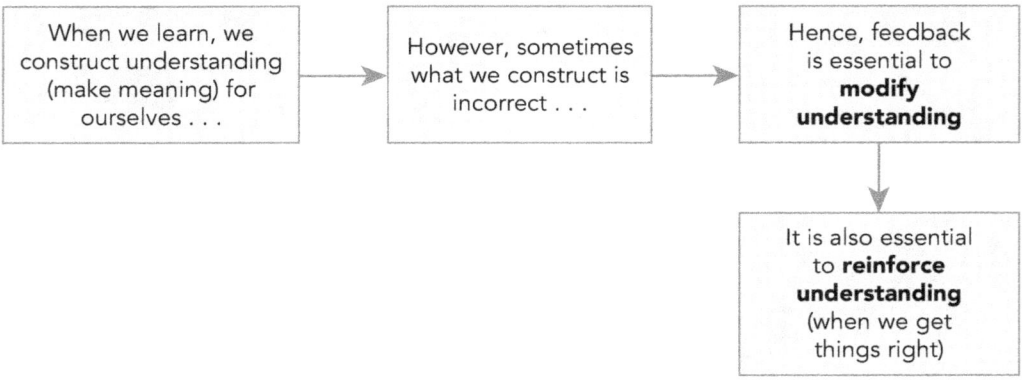

**FIGURE 12-2.** Feedback and constructive learning

# INSTRUCTIONAL CONSIDERATIONS

Unfortunately, many teachers working in higher education think feedback applies only to the summative assessment process and focus on the products of learning at the end of a unit of instruction.

However, as this book has demonstrated several times, feedback is integral to the process of learning and therefore must be applied whenever a learner is required to practice various cognitive and practical skills, usually as part of learning activities. Feedback-corrected practice, summarized in Figure 12-3 (from Chapter 10), must happen in all instructional contexts, since it allows learners to apply feedback directly as they are attempting to learn skills. Evaluation activities, a key aspect of the Roadmap for Teaching, should be included in the design of instructional experiences in an ongoing fashion to check whether a learner has achieved a learning goal. They also provide another important outlet for feedback. As you can see, feedback should be designed into the instructional experience as a core component. Frequently, though, it isn't!

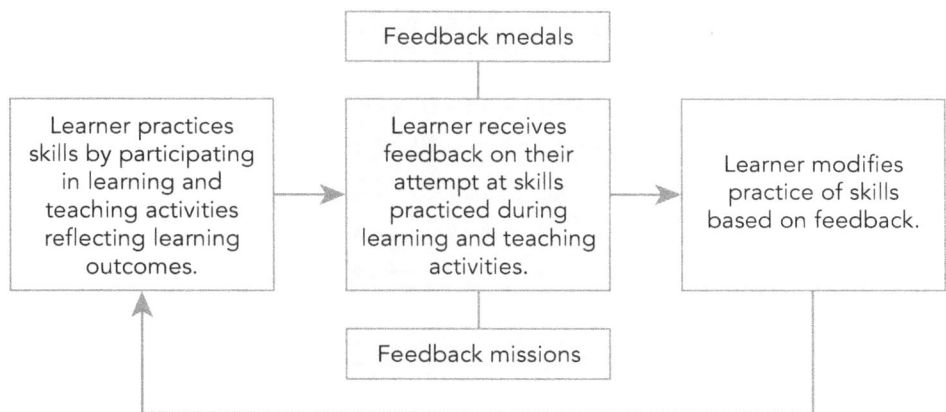

**FIGURE 12-3.** Feedback-corrected practice

There is some evidence to suggest that learners working on higher-order cognitive skills, as they generally will be during the Cheese Sandwich process (see Chapter 7), benefit from being allowed time to process whatever task they're engaged in before feedback is provided (Shute, 2008). This is similar to what Phil Race has labeled *making sense* in his Ripples on a Pond model (Race, 2019). Hence, when learners are working on higher-order skills, it's important to give them time to make sense of what they are doing before applying feedback.

As covered in Chapters 4 and 9, the starting point for the Roadmap for Teaching is the creation of clear, measurable learning outcomes. Learning outcomes represent the goals of learning for the learners and play a very important role in the effective application of feedback. For example, work by Butler and Winne (1995) demonstrated that learner perceptions of and, critically, receptiveness to feedback are strongly related to the presence of learning outcomes. In short, learners are more receptive to feedback if they can clearly see how it is helping them to move toward a learning outcome or goal. Hence, ensuring learning is goal-directed is vital to how well feedback is received by learners, especially if the outcomes are challenging and supported by feedback, which in turn supports motivation, effort, and persistence—core elements of the UDL principle of engagement.

The kind of feedback that we embed into the Roadmap for Teaching is used solely to improve learning. It is delivered in a timely fashion because learners receive it as they practice important cognitive and practical skills as part of their instructional experiences. It takes place during the learning process, focusing on aspects of learning that are relevant to that specific moment (not a summative assessment that was completed weeks previously and since forgotten about), with opportunities for learners to discuss and unpack the feedback with the feedback provider, whether that's their teacher, their peers, or even themselves. This process largely aligns to what we know in UDL terms as *mastery-oriented feedback.*

Mastery-oriented feedback is just that—feedback that supports the development of learner mastery over learning, as opposed to feedback that reflects performance against a fixed benchmark. It espouses the importance of effort, persistence, practice, process, and progress in relation to learning outcomes, and it's geared toward supporting the development of effective long-term learning habits and practices. Remember, part of being an expert learner is recognizing how one personally achieves mastery over learning content; thus, mastery-oriented feedback supports learners in recognizing their personal means of achieving learning outcomes. Mastery-oriented feedback should:

- Support self-awareness, efficacy development, perseverance, and the application of specific support strategies when challenges are faced.

- Emphasize the learning journey, effort, distance traveled (improvement), and achieving mastery over learning, rather than getting a good grade.

- Be specific to given tasks/skills, happen whenever learners are required to respond to a learning stimulus, and occur frequently.

- Inform progress toward personal mastery of learning outcomes as opposed to being comparative to other learners.

- Provide self-evaluation skills, allowing learners to spot their own errors and omissions.

## MEDALS AND MISSIONS

As mentioned in Chapter 10, when you are providing feedback as part of instructional experiences to support the development of learning mastery, it is important to use feedback "medals" and feedback "missions" (Petty, 2014).

### Medals

A feedback medal tells the learner what they did well when participating in a learning activity or responding to a learning stimulus. The critical feature of the medal is that it provides information on *why* the learner did well in responding to a learning stimulus or learning activity. Learners may not always be aware why they have done something well. Therefore, it's very important to make them aware so that they can build up a toolkit of effective learning habits and practices that they can use again in the future. Feedback medals can be provided on the *products* of learning, or an actual output or performance on a skill or task related to the learning outcomes. A summative assessment output would represent a "product" of learning.

Medals can also be provided on the *process* of learning, which may involve giving feedback on the approach a learner used on some task related to a learning goal, or on how well a learner used various learning resources or how well organized they were. It could even include feedback on how well engaged the learner was in the task, including their level of perseverance in the face of challenge. To use a sports analogy, feedback on the process of learning is akin to giving feedback on the performance, irrespective of the result, of an athlete or team during a game. Conversely, feedback on the products of learning is akin to giving feedback on the result rather than the performance. The sports analogy is useful because athletes and sports teams frequently perform well despite losing. Even in defeat, knowing that they gave a good performance can give them the confidence and belief they need to approach the next game with the optimum level of motivation and application. Learning can operate in much the same way.

Finally, medals can be provided on learning *progress*. Progress medals are exactly what the name implies—they provide information on the progress learners are making against learning outcomes. To return to an analogy used earlier in the book, imagine going on a long car journey without knowing your destination; you wouldn't know how far you've traveled at any point or how far you have left to go. How would you feel? What impact would this have on your motivation and persistence? Would you need to stop for fuel, food, or water? Would you need a rest break? Fuel, food, water, and rest breaks represent things that may support your progress on your journey. Providing feedback on learning progress supports learner motivation and lets learners know if they need to obtain anything that may support them on their journey, such as specific strategies or resources, especially when they face challenges. Feedback medals should always include product, process, and progress medals.

## Missions

A feedback mission tells the learner what they could improve upon when participating in a learning activity or responding to a learning stimulus. The critical feature of the mission is that it also provides information on *how* the learner can improve, because it's quite likely that they won't know how to do so for themselves. Again, providing learners with clear information on how to improve is part of how they develop a toolkit of effective learning habits and practices they can use again in the future, and supports their continued growth so that they can learn effectively and independently.

As above, feedback missions can be provided on the learning products, process, or progress. Regardless of their dimension, feedback missions should always be forward-looking and positive and should come across more like advice than criticism (Petty, 2014) to support continued learner motivation, effort, and persistence. Missions should, where possible, include information on self-evaluation skills so that the learner can spot their own errors and omissions. If a learner can't self-evaluate, it's very difficult for them to improve their learning—particularly in higher education, where much of the learning experience is self-directed and independent. A feedback mission narrows the gap between where the learner currently is in terms of their learning and where they need to be. Thus, missions are critical for learners in setting personal learning goals and continually developing personal learning expertise.

You may be thinking, *This seems like a big ask to fit mastery-oriented feedback with medals and missions into single instructional experiences.* However, this is one of the key reasons why the Cheese Sandwich (Chapter 7) repurposes the time learners spend with their teachers and peers: There's more time and opportunity to support learning with mastery-oriented feedback.

When providing mastery-oriented feedback with medals and missions (and all the characteristics inherent within them), you'll have to decide what's the most appropriate feedback for any given learning scenario. Whether you give medals based on product, process, or progress, or whether your feedback is mission based and includes information on how to self-evaluate, for example, will largely depend on the situation and learners in question. For the teacher, mastery-oriented feedback, medals, and missions are like tools in a toolkit. As a teacher, you should be able to use these tools proficiently, but the real skill in teaching is being able to select the right skill for the job in any given scenario. Being able to do this will depend on knowing your learners, knowing their strengths and challenges, and knowing what will serve them best at various points in their learning journey. Again, the Cheese Sandwich emphasizes the time teachers spend with their learners so that teachers can get to know their learners better and thus support their learning more effectively. In addition, it's important to remember that you, as the teacher, aren't the only source of feedback available.

## TRIANGULATED FEEDBACK

A critical feature of the Cheese Sandwich is that it emphasizes the time learners spend with their teachers and their peers. This is because as well as leveraging teacher support to a greater extent than more traditional models of higher education, in the Cheese Sandwich model learners also leverage the support of their peers. In fact, the Cheese Sandwich actively encourages learners to assess and provide feedback to their peers in reciprocal fashion. The benefits of this are twofold: Not only do the learners gain another source of feedback aside from the teacher, but they also develop important evaluative skills by assessing and giving feedback to each other, which they can use to support their own learning. The Cheese Sandwich also emphasizes the need for learners to self-assess and self-evaluate so that they can be a source of feedback to themselves. Self-evaluation and the feedback it provides reflect the central ideas and purpose of the assessment *as* learning strategies addressed in Chapter 11.

It is important to teach learners about the importance of feedback for their ongoing learning such that they should be encouraged to become *feedback seekers*, intentionally looking out for opportunities where they can receive feedback on their learning, even in self-directed study. In this respect, learners can surround themselves with a *feedback cage*, a network of people from whom they can receive valuable feedback on their learning; see Figure 12-4, where the arrows showing feedback being directed toward the learner. This can be self-directed (curved arrow) or it can come from teachers, peers, and other sources, such as general learning support services, often found in university libraries, or specialist support services (if a learner was dyslexic, for example). Depending on the nature of the subject studied, feedback could come from employers, industry figures, or even professional bodies. The possibilities for learners to receive feedback from numerous sources in triangulated fashion are often more abundant than we might think.

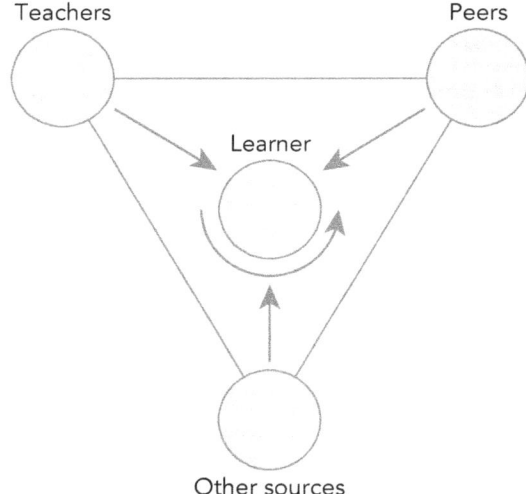

**FIGURE 12-4.** The feedback cage

**PAUSE AND THINK** Do you currently include opportunities to receive and give feedback as part of your instructional experiences or teaching sessions? Who provides feedback to your learners during instructional experiences or teaching sessions? Does each learner receive medals and missions relating to their learning?

# 13

## A Word on Technology

My original plan for this book did not include a chapter specifically focused on the role and use of technology in designing and delivering instructional experiences according to the UDL principles. The main reason for this was because UDL isn't dependent on technology. Just because we utilize various forms of technology in the design and delivery of instructional experiences doesn't mean they have been well designed or even universally designed. Unfortunately, I've seen this in my own experiences of supporting others to implement UDL, with colleagues assuming they'd implemented UDL just because they had recorded their lectures, paying very little attention to embedding the UDL principles elsewhere in the session design or delivery.

It's also a bit of a bugbear of mine that many teachers feel the need to tick the technology box—to include technology in their instructional designs because they feel they should, rather than because it is genuinely reducing or removing barriers and thus supporting learners to effectively meet learning outcomes. I've observed many teaching sessions that include an endless raft of technological tools that add little value to the learning experience. Subsequently, I've always felt it important to master teaching, and indeed UDL, in relatively low-tech ways before embarking on the use of more sophisticated technological applications. We must learn to walk before we can run.

However, since technology plays such a dominant role in our lives generally, and in education more specifically, I felt it would be remiss of me not to cover the role and use of technology in designing instructional experiences, particularly accessible, inclusive, and equitable ones in line with UDL. In addition, I've espoused the use of various technological applications as part of the Cheese Sandwich when discussing how multimedia options—such as screencasts, videos, and podcasts—can represent valuable ways to deliver content. Hence, I would be doing my readers a disservice if I did not specifically address technology in terms of instructional design.

## DESIGNING FOR THOSE IN THE MARGINS BENEFITS EVERYONE

A common UDL idea is that if we design for those learners in the margins, then it benefits all learners. Technology encapsulates this idea very well. For example, many universities now make video recordings of classes available to learners, a practice that in many institutions was initially a means of supporting learners with declared disabilities. For example, some learners—such as those with physical or mobility difficulties, learners with dyslexia, or learners who experience fatigue due to the effects of a disability or long-term condition—may find taking written notes in class challenging. Recording classes benefits such learners because it considerably reduces the requirement to take notes. However, recording classes in this way also hugely benefits learners who do not have a disability. For example, recording classes benefits the learner who can't make it to class because they have child care responsibilities, or the learner who is required to work during class hours, or even the learner who just wants to deepen their understanding of content by watching the recording several times. These scenarios demonstrate how a technological benefit used to reduce or remove barriers for learners with disabilities in fact benefits all learners.

Another example of how designing for those in the margins benefits everyone concerns the use of assistive technology or software during learning scenarios. Unfortunately, assistive software is often incorrectly characterized as being for disabled learners only, with many teachers unaware of its potential benefits for all learners. For example, for those learners who find writing challenging, such as those with dyslexia, dysgraphia, or a physical difficulty that affects their fine motor skills, speech-to-text software (a technology that converts speech into written text) can help to remove or reduce barriers posed by the requirement to write. Learners can write notes, essays, reports, or any other text-based output by speaking rather than writing, reducing or removing a barrier to learning. However, speech-to-text software can also benefit learners without disabilities. For example, consider a learner who is a better orator than writer and has been tasked with creating an essay plan. This learner could potentially benefit from speech-to-text software to help them summarize their ideas, plan, and even write the essay, which could be a challenge for any learner who finds writing difficult.

Graphic organizer software has often been recommended as a learning resource for those with learning disabilities (LD; Dexter & Hughes, 2011). For example, learners with LD frequently have difficulties with core academic skills such as reading, as well as with essential skills for study, including being able to connect new learning to prior knowledge, recognize irrelevant information, identify key ideas and related concepts, make inferences, and develop strategies to solve problems (Dexter & Hughes, 2011). Graphic organizers present ideas and information visually to enable learners to comprehend the relationships between concepts and facts in a clearer and more understandable manner. The purpose of a graphic organizer is to support learning by making complex ideas and concepts easier to make sense of, helping learners make connections between new and existing learning.

There are various types of graphic organizers—mind maps, spider maps, Venn diagrams, and sequence charts, to name a few—and software to help learners create them. As a result, graphic organizers seem well suited to the needs of learners with LD. However, one could argue that the particular learning challenges faced by learners with LD represent hurdles for all learners to an extent (Dexter, Park, & Hughes, 2011), so using graphic organizer software could be beneficial for all learners.

With some support, training, coaching, and guidance, all learners can use various assistive technologies and software to support their learning in a way that removes or reduces barriers. It's important to remember that they may need support with optimizing the use of such technologies, as it's unlikely that they will have used them previously, especially if they don't have a disability. Once they can use assistive technology proficiently, they can transfer their skills in using the software to different contexts, particularly employment contexts, such as writing cover letters, resumes, or employment applications. Using technology as part of their learning experience can support learners in their pursuit of lifelong learning.

**PAUSE AND THINK** Do you currently encourage your learners to use assistive technology or software? Do you know of any assistive technology or software that could support all learners in your context?

## SETTING THE RECORD STRAIGHT

At its heart, UDL is a design framework that accounts for the variability among all learners, supporting them to learn effectively by providing them with multiple learning pathways that remove or reduce barriers to learning. There is no prerequisite for technology to be part of this process. As Jodie Black and Eric Moore have stated so eloquently in their excellent book *UDL Navigators in Higher Education*, the relationship between UDL and technology should be complementary rather than codependent, and therefore one could effectively apply universal design in low- or even no-tech ways (Black & Moore, 2019). However, it's important that we think about the nature of the learners we are supporting right now in higher education and those we will be supporting in the future. As detailed in Chapter 1, modern higher education learners largely consist of those who have experienced technology since birth, growing up in a world in which individualism, personalization, and customizability are the normal byproducts of advances in technology. A large proportion of higher education learners have spent their teenage years hardwired to the internet via a mobile device such as a tablet or smartphone. As a result, they might assume that technology is an inherent part of the learning experience, offering the individualism, personalization, and customizability they have come to expect everywhere else.

## THE BENEFITS OF TECHNOLOGY

As well as possibly being an expectation of many higher education learners today, technology also has the potential to enhance the accessibility and flexibility of how they experience and engage with learning. For example, technology enables learners to adapt and modify learning resources and materials in ways that are customizable to their preferences, as well as helping them to remove or reduce important accessibility barriers by changing font sizes, styles, colors, backgrounds, layouts, and the need for printed materials.

From a teaching perspective, the use of technology can also help to lighten the load on teachers. When instructional experiences are designed and delivered in low- or no-tech fashion, teachers must work even harder to provide the multiple learning pathways characteristic of a UDL approach in terms of instructional approaches, learning resources, and the ways in which learners demonstrate their learning. In contrast, an instructional experience that is designed and delivered utilizing technology enables a greater level of choice and autonomy in relation to how learners access, adapt, and modify learning content and the resources that support it, as well as how they approach and engage with various learning tasks. For example, it is far easier for the teacher to provide online learning materials that learners can modify according to their needs and preferences in advance of instructional experiences than it is for the teacher to create multiple types of hard copy to distribute physically during a teaching session in order to accommodate learner variability. Hence, technology often affords teachers many efficiencies in terms of designing instructional experiences, creating the resources that support them, and delivering them. Note that technology also enables greater options from a UDL perspective. For example, it's easier to provide multiple means of engagement, representation, and action and expression if technological means are included in the instructional design. In other words, incorporating technology into instructional designs can sometimes make it easier to create the different learning pathways that remove or reduce barriers to the achievement of learning outcomes.

## COMMON ASSUMPTIONS

Since many learners in modern higher education settings have grown up with technology—using it for everyday pursuits, such as watching television, listening to music, shopping, and communicating with friends—many teachers assume that those learners will naturally be skilled at using it for learning, without the need for support or practice. Indeed, in society more generally there seems to be a mistaken belief that young people by definition must be highly experienced and skilled in the use of technology in all scenarios. Terms like "digital natives" have been used for the better part of the last decade to define the generation who have grown up with technology since birth or childhood. Frankly, such terms are unhelpful since they promote the stereotype that all young people, including higher education learners, can perform magic with mobile smart devices and computers. Thus, when contemplating the use of technologies as part of our learning designs, we must ask ourselves whether the learners can access and use the technology adequately for its intended purpose. If we decide that some or all of the learners may not be able to use or access the technology adequately to meet its purpose, then next we must consider how we can support them to do so with training, coaching, and guidance. As you can see, we can't just throw technology into our learning designs; we must carefully consider its purpose, as well as learner access to and proficiency with it.

A second common assumption concerns the learners' level of access to technology, particularly when they are learning online and in remote settings. This has been a particular issue throughout the COVID-19 pandemic, in which learning shifted almost entirely online.

According to the regulatory body for English higher education, the Office for Students, *digital poverty* is an inability to fully engage and interact with the digital world (OfS, 2020). Unfortunately, it can be a very real problem for many higher education learners, as we saw during the COVID pandemic. From a learning perspective, digital poverty can happen for a variety of reasons, most of which reflect a lack of access to the technological infrastructure considered core to learning in online scenarios, including

- appropriate study spaces;
- appropriate hardware;
- appropriate software;
- reliable internet access;
- trained instructors; and
- technical support.

If learners have difficulty accessing any of these items, they are said to be experiencing digital poverty (OfS, 2020). As teachers, the extent to which we can improve access to the items may be quite limited. However, there are some things we can do to support learners experiencing digital poverty. As a starting point, it is important that we at least consider issues around access to technologies, particularly in online learning scenarios, and the potential impact of digital poverty among learners.

## THINGS WE CAN DO

In online learning scenarios—say, during synchronous teaching sessions, which were perhaps the central approach to learning and teaching during the pandemic—learners often require high-speed internet connections, with audio and video applications also likely to require higher-bandwidth connections. For a learner experiencing digital poverty, access to high connection speeds and bandwidths may pose problems. Furthermore, it may also be a challenge for a learner to find a suitable space (that is, quiet and free from distractions) to participate in a synchronous session. To address the potential burden of digital poverty when teaching online, we must think about how important learning from a session like this could be delivered using alternative means and learning resources. For example, important learning points from the synchronous session could be captured as a short podcast or screencast, which could be downloaded to a mobile smart device. Placing the key learning points into a shortened, downloadable format attenuates the need for livestreaming, which generally requires a fast and powerful internet connection and/or large amounts of mobile data. Being able to listen to or watch the key learning points through a mobile device via earphones also reduces the need for a personal study space free from distraction.

Mobile devices, particularly mobile phones, represent the principal way in which the iGeneration (Twenge, 2017), introduced in Chapter 1, access the internet. Among the iGeneration, according to the German marketing and consumer data company Statista (2022), approximately 98 percent have access to a smartphone. And, according to Ofcom (2018), the UK government–approved regulatory and competition authority for broadcasting and telecommunications, a fifth of this age group spends up to seven hours per day using their phone. Given the centrality of the mobile phone in the lives of many modern students, we can't overlook its position as a key mechanism for engaging with learning. If the aforementioned podcast/screencast learning resources were provided in advance of the synchronous session alongside other learning resources that can be easily accessed, such as slides, glossaries, images, and summaries, then learners would have access to a variety of resources that will further support their learning, despite their participation in the synchronous learning aspects being potentially limited.

There are, of course, other ways in which access to learning could be enabled in the scenario just described. The point, though, is that we must always think about potential barriers between learners and their learning, and work to reduce or remove them. In the previous example, alternative learning pathways are provided to reduce the barriers posed by digital poverty. This is what UDL is essentially all about: creating alternative learning pathways to remove or reduce barriers to learning.

**PAUSE AND THINK** Think about your current practice. Does the way in which you utilize technology present any barriers to your learners? If so, how can you reduce or remove them?

## CLEAR, INTENTIONAL PURPOSE

I think we're past the debate as to whether the use of technology in higher education is good or bad or whether it works or not. Technology is here to stay, so we'd better find a way of working with it. The key question is *how* we're using technology rather than *whether* we're using it. We must ask ourselves how technology is being used in the design of our instructional experiences to support achievement of learning outcomes in an intentional way. The goal always comes before the means of achieving it. As mentioned earlier in this chapter, we must avoid the temptation to use technology in our instructional designs simply for the sake of it. There must be a clear purpose for its inclusion.

A useful starting point when thinking about the inclusion of technology in your instructional designs is to refer back to the Roadmap for Teaching introduced in Chapter 5. For example, will your learning outcomes be about mastering a particular technology, such as statistical analysis software or a research database? Will you require certain technologies to support the learning activities you include in your designs as a learning resource (such as an online glossary) or as the means to complete an activity (such as a mobile voting application)? Will you use technology to provide feedback by using a recording application to provide audio feedback? Will you use technology to evaluate learner understanding by, say, using an online submission portal?

Whatever way you use technology, it must support achievement of the learning outcomes. Learning outcomes are non-negotiable, but the learning activities and feedback that support their achievement, as well as the evaluation activities that evaluate whether learners have met the learning outcomes, should be varied to reflect the variability of your learners. Part of that variation might include the use of technological innovations. Once we've established clear learning outcomes, we can then use backward design, as discussed in Chapter 5, to create the pathways that support the achievement of the learning outcomes.

The different pathways you create for learners to achieve learning outcomes may include technology as a means of reducing or removing barriers. Likewise, it's vital to remember that technology, however it is deployed, must support the achievement of learning outcomes.

**PAUSE AND THINK** Think about how you currently utilize technology. Does your utilization of technology clearly support learners to achieve the learning outcomes? If not, why not? Can you use technology in a more effective way to support learner achievement of the learning outcomes?

Remember that your learners must be able to access and use whatever technology you incorporate into your instructional design for its intended purpose, as described earlier in this chapter.

---

### QUICK-START GUIDE: ACCESSIBLE RESOURCES AND MATERIALS

Here are some quick tips to making common technology-based educational resources and materials more accessible. Note that the advice and guidance provided does not represent an exhaustive foray into making all technology-based educational materials more accessible. The advice and guidance provided is intended to be quick and easy, as opposed to the definitive accessibility guide, but should nonetheless serve as a useful starting point.

**POWERPOINT SLIDES**

1. Have slides in the correct order.

    Ensure your slides are in the correct reading order to enable screen reading software to read them aloud correctly.

2. Arrange slide content in a logical reading order.

    Make sure objects/items on each slide are arranged in a logical reading order to allow screen reading software to read them aloud in the right order. To set the reading order, do the following:

    a. Click **Home** in PowerPoint.

    b. Select **Arrange** from the ribbon.

    c. Select **Reading Pane**.

    d. Select the reading order of items/objects in the selection pane as appropriate.

3. Format tables, figures, and images clearly.

   Tables should be presented in a simple "grid" structure, with column headers. Nested tables, merged cells, and blank columns or rows should be avoided, as they can make it difficult for screen readers to read them. Include alternative text descriptions for all tables for screen reader users.

   Include figures and images where appropriate, as they support learner interpretation of content. Place figures and images separate from any text, with sufficient space between them, as opposed to wrapping text around figures and images. Include alternative text descriptions of images and figures for screen readers.

4. Use simple and straightforward language.

   Language should be understandable to the reader or listener the first time they read or hear it. Keep sentences short, use active rather than passive voice, use bullet points where necessary, and avoid jargon and acronyms where possible.

5. Use slide titles and headings.

   Slide titles and headings enable screen readers to easily identify and navigate the slideshow presentation for listeners based on the titles and headings.

6. Make your presentation and layout easily legible.

   Use a sans serif font like Arial or Verdana in a large type size (28-point type is a good minimum), with 1.5 line spacing and text left justified. Ensure high contrast between background and font. Pastel backgrounds, such as cream or yellow, work well with black text, for example. Use bold font for emphasis as opposed to underlining, italics, or color. Avoid long paragraphs. Make sure your text is easily readable, and limit the text/number of lines in each slide. Consider the "6 by 7" rule: six words per line, seven lines per slide.

7. Use speaker notes.

   Provide further or more in-depth information by including speaker notes. Share your slides in advance of teaching sessions (at least 48 hours) so that your audience can refer to the slides and notes both before and after the presentation. If slides are used for recorded presentations, then scripted speaker notes can also function as a transcript.

8. Use alternative formats.

   To ensure optimum accessibility, save and share your slides in alternative formats compatible with screen readers, such as Word documents (which can be saved as handouts) or PDF files.

9. Use the PowerPoint accessibility checker.

   PowerPoint has a built-in accessibility checker in the Review menu on the ribbon. You can create a slideshow with the accessibility checker on so that you can ensure it's accessible as you create it, or you can check the slideshow's accessibility once it is complete. Either way, the checker will inform you of any accessibility issues with suggestions on how to fix them.

**VIDEOS**

1. Check your learning management system.

   As an educator it is likely that you'll host video and audio content through your institution's learning management system (LMS). Hopefully, the LMS you use will include accessibility features and align with the Web Content Accessibility Guidelines (WCAG), a specific set of standards intended to make websites more accessible to people with disabilities, but it's best to confirm this. It's also worth checking that the media player you intend to use to play video and audio content through the LMS includes basic accessibility features, such as clearly labeled player controls (play, pause, stop, etc.); does not autoplay; and can be navigated and activated via keyboard controls.

2. Use closed captions.

   *Captioning* is the display of text on a video to represent the audio content. It mostly indicates the video dialogue, but it may also describe music, sound effects, and the like. Closed captions allow learners to choose to have the captions displayed or not when watching a video. Closed captions are identified by a [CC] icon and are the most common form of captioning.

3. Provide a transcript.

   A *transcript* is a written record of all of the dialogue in a video. Sometimes when videos are recorded for PowerPoint presentations, it can be useful to provide the transcript for each slide in the notes section, as it makes it easier to match the dialogue to content on the slides. A separate transcript can also be provided.

4. Provide media alternative transcript if necessary.

   *Media alternative transcript* provides a text description of what's being shown on a video in addition to any dialogue. For example, a character in a video may look sad but not be saying anything. With media alternative transcript, learners would get a text description of the character's sad expression despite the lack of dialogue.

5. Provide standard audio description if necessary.

   *Standard audio description* provides descriptive audio narration for any visual elements in videos that don't have an audio track. For example, a video about teaching may show a teacher in a lecture hall answering questions but with no audio narration. With standard audio description, the shot would be accompanied by some narration like "A teacher answers student questions in a lecture hall" or similar.

6. Provide extended audio description if necessary.

   *Extended audio description* involves intentionally pausing a video to provide extended descriptive audio narration for any visual elements in videos without an audio track. This is often necessary if the visual elements without an audio track are very short. Returning to the previous example of the visual shot of a teacher in a lecture hall, extended audio description may include narration like "First-year students in a biology class raise their hands to ask questions about their upcoming exam. Their teacher selects a student in the front row to respond to" or similar.

**PODCASTS**

1. Check your learning management system.

   As with videos, it's important to ensure that your LMS aligns with WCAG standards, and that the media player you intend to use includes basic accessibility features, such as clearly labeled player controls (play, pause, stop, etc.); does not autoplay; and can be navigated and activated via keyboard controls.

2. Provide a transcript.

   Just as you would for a video, make sure you provide a written record of all the dialogue in a podcast via a transcript. The transcript can then be linked to the podcast via the LMS.

3. Offer alternative formats.

   Podcast content can often be easily repurposed for different formats. For example, audio recorded for a podcast can be uploaded to YouTube. In such a case you might also include a logo or image to go with the audio recording in place of any video content. You could also include a video recording of your podcast, or a "vodcast," which is a format many radio stations use for their podcasts. If using video, make sure you include closed captions.

4. Ensure clear audio.

   Sometimes it's beneficial for podcast participants to wear a microphone to prevent poor or inconsistent sound quality. For example, the audio on podcasts recorded on web conferencing software might be affected by how far the person sits from their computer screen. If they move backward (farther from the screen) and then forward (closer to the screen), the audio is often inconsistent, especially in terms of volume. It can also be useful for participants to speak one at a time (not over each other), and for the participants in listening mode to mute their microphones to eliminate background noise.

**WORD DOCUMENTS**

1. Use simple and straightforward language.

   Language should be understandable to the reader or listener the first time they read or hear it. For example, keep sentences short, use active rather than passive voice, use bullet points where necessary, and avoid jargon and acronyms where possible.

2. Use appropriate headings.

   Always use Word's built-in hierarchy of headings (Heading 1, Heading 2, etc.) because screen readers can use them to easily identify and navigate documents for listeners.

3. Make your presentation and layout easily legible.

   Use a sans serif font like Arial or Verdana in 12- to 14-point type with 1.5 line spacing and text left justified. Ensure high contrast between the background and font. Pastel backgrounds, such as cream or yellow, work well with black text, for example. Use bold font for emphasis as opposed to underlining, italics, or color. Avoid long paragraphs and leave a clear space between paragraphs.

4. Format tables, figures, and images clearly.

   Tables should be presented in a simple "grid" structure, with column headers. Avoid nested tables, merged cells, and blank columns or rows, as they make it difficult for screen readers to read tables. Include alternative text descriptions for all tables for screen reader users.

   Include figures and images where appropriate, as they support learner interpretation of content. Place figures and images separate from text with sufficient space between them, as opposed to wrapping text around figures and images. Include alternative text descriptions of images for screen readers.

5. Use intuitive hyperlinks.

   If you link to other resources, avoid vague phrases like "click here" in favor of descriptive text hyperlinks, such as "Find articles by searching the university catalog" or similar. It can be useful to include the full URL of a linked resource in brackets after the link to make it available should the document be printed.

6. Use the Word accessibility checker.

   Word has a built-in accessibility checker in the Review menu on the ribbon. You can create a document with the accessibility checker on so that you can ensure it's accessible as you create it, or you can check the accessibility of your document once it is complete. Either way, the checker will inform you of any accessibility issues with suggestions on how to fix them.

## PDF FILES (CONVERTING FROM WORD AND POWERPOINT)

1. Follow the golden rules.

   PDF documents often begin in other applications, such as Word or PowerPoint. Therefore, you should optimize the accessibility of the source document before converting it to a PDF. If you're converting a PDF from a Word document, for example, the first step is to adhere to the accessibility steps for Word documents just described. If you're converting from PowerPoint, first make sure you adhere to the accessibility steps for PowerPoint slides listed earlier.

2. Convert for accessibility.

   To be accessible, PDFs must be "tagged." Tags give assistive technologies, such as screen readers, information about the document's content and are important from a structural perspective. Tags are not generally visible in the document. Some common tags are heading tags (<h>), image tags (<figure>), and paragraph tags (<p>).

3. Follow the appropriate steps for conversion.

   When converting your Word or PowerPoint document to PDF, use the following steps:

   a. In your Word/PowerPoint document, click **File**.

   b. Select **Save As**.

   c. Open the File Explorer by clicking **Browse**.

   d. From the **Save as type** drop-down menu, select **PDF**.

   e. Click **Options**.

   f. Select **Document structure tags for accessibility**.

   g. Click **OK** to save the file in your specified location.

## PDF DOCUMENTS (FROM SCANNED MATERIALS)

1. Use optical character recognition (OCR).

   PDFs created by scanning an existing document are initially unreadable by screen readers because the scan is an image. Therefore, you'll need to use optical character recognition (OCR) to make the PDFs editable and readable by screen readers. If using applications such as Adobe Acrobat, you can automatically apply OCR to the scanned document by clicking Edit PDF tool in the right pane. Adobe Acrobat itself has a "read aloud" function as well.

2. Use the Make Accessible function.

   Adobe Acrobat also has a Make Accessible function that enables you to optimize PDFs for accessibility. To use the Make Accessible function in Adobe Acrobat, follow these steps:

   a. In Adobe Acrobat select **Tools**.

   b. Then select **Action Wizard**, which opens the Action Wizard toolset in a separate toolbar.

> c. Select **Make Accessible** from the Actions List.
>
> d. Select the documents you want to make accessible.
>
> e. Select **Start**.
>
> Follow the Make Accessible prompts to optimize the accessibility of your PDF.

# Part IV

# Mastery in Action

# 14

## Putting It All Together

Now that you have learned about all of the parts of the Roadmap for Teaching and how to implement each most effectively as part of the Cheese Sandwich approach, it's time to think about how you can plan them into the design of your instructional experiences.

We shouldn't forget that, at its core, UDL is about design; the clue is right there in the name. Of course, design can refer to many things, such as the design of teaching activities, resources, assessments, or even individual units or entire programs of learning. However, in this particular context, we're interested in the design of instructional experiences, or *instructional design*.

Based on everything covered in this book so far, there are several key elements that must be included in instructional design to support effective mastery over learning and subsequent expert learning:

- A means of assessing learner variability (especially if you're teaching a new group for the first time), or at least including learner variability considerations into the design of your instructional experiences

- The elements of the Roadmap for Teaching (learning outcomes, learning activities, evaluation activities, and opportunities for feedback), with each implemented according to the advice given

- Emphasis on teacher and peer support of content mastery rather than content transmission

- Application of the UDL principles in response to learner variability
- Learner feedback considerations

Table 14-1 lists a number of important questions relating to these elements. You can use it as a basic starting point to ensure you have covered the core considerations for instructional design.

**TABLE 14-1.** Important Considerations for Instructional Design

| Knowing your learners | |
|---|---|
| • Do you know about the variability of your learners? | |
| • What barriers are your learners likely to face? | |
| • How are you assessing the variability of your learners? | |
| • What tools and techniques will you use? | |
| **Roadmap for Teaching** | |
| • What are your learning goals or outcomes? | |
| • What do the learners need to know or be able to do as a result of their learning? | |
| • What learning activities will you use? | |
| • Do they reflect the learning goals or outcomes? | |
| • How will the activities enable the learners to master the cognitive skills articulated in the learning goals or outcomes? | |
| • How are you evaluating learner achievement of the learning goals or outcomes? | |
| • Does the evaluation reflect the learning goals or outcomes? | |
| • When, where, and how is feedback being provided to learners? | |

| UDL | |
|---|---|
| • How are you providing multiple learning pathways to support achievement of the learning goals or outcomes using the UDL principles? How are you implementing multiple means of engagement, representation, and action and expression? | |
| • How are you responding to learner variability using the UDL principles? | |
| • How are you getting feedback from your learners and how often? | |
| • How will you action learner feedback? | |

Fitting all of these considerations into your instructional design may seem like a daunting prospect. Fortunately, there is a process for doing just that: CUTLAS, which stands for Creating Universal Teaching Learning and Assessment Strategies (Merry, 2019; 2021). CUTLAS is a structured process that teachers can work through to help them design learning experiences. Essentially, the CUTLAS process supports teachers with the intentional design of learning experiences underpinned by the UDL principles and containing all of the key design elements discussed in this book, particularly the Cheese Sandwich discussed in Chapter 7. CUTLAS embeds UDL into the learning design process, ensuring that the principles of UDL—engagement, representation, and action and expression—are given extensive consideration at the time of instructional design, and thus become pillars of the design process, rather than bolted-on "tips and tricks" (as they unfortunately can be if added to an existing design).

CUTLAS was developed from two similar learning design processes. The first is the *Carpe Diem* learning design methodology, an approach to designing constructively aligned, technology-enhanced learning experiences (Armellini & Jones, 2008; Salmon, Jones and Armellini, 2008). The idea behind Carpe Diem is that every moment of time during the learning design process is spent on designing a curriculum that can be put into immediate use with learners—hence the name, which is Latin for "seize the day." The second approach influencing CUTLAS is *CAIeRO* (Creating Aligned, Interactive, educational Resource Opportunities; Usher,

McNeill, & Creanor, 2018), developed by the University of Northampton in the UK. Both approaches utilize clear, outcomes-driven approaches to designing learning experiences and include critical constituents of the learning design process, such as learning outcomes, assessments/evaluations, learner and teacher activities, and required resources.

CUTLAS is based on the principles of backward design, in which we set the goals or outcomes of learning before defining the evaluation or assessment and instructional strategies that support achievement of those goals. Backward design is discussed in Chapters 5 and 9.

The CUTLAS process began as a means of creating units or modules of learning and/or entire programs of learning. It was created to support the *design down* (starting at the program level), *deliver up* (from the classroom upward) approach that is so important to university-wide UDL implementation (Black & Moore, 2019). However, it quickly became obvious that CUTLAS could be effectively used to create individual learning experiences too. Thus, CUTLAS can be used as an instructional design and planning tool, but with a few additional elements.

When using CUTLAS to create an individual learning experience, you use the Cheese Sandwich approach. Remember from Chapter 7 that in the Cheese Sandwich, the process of learners achieving learning outcomes or goals is extended across three phases: 1) self-directed learning that happens before learners learn with direct support from teachers and peers; 2) learning that is directly supported by teachers and peers; and 3) self-directed learning that happens after learners learn with direct support from teachers and peers. Hence, rather than being used to plan a single teaching session, CUTLAS supports teachers to plan a block of learning according to the Cheese Sandwich approach. Remember that a "block of learning" in this context is all of the learning and teaching activity that supports the learning of a given topic or content area, several aspects of which happen beyond the classroom or at times when learners and teachers are together, be it physically or virtually. Hence, we're not really planning sessions or lessons, we're planning the way in which learners learn entire topics.

## THE FOUR STAGES OF CUTLAS

There are four stages to CUTLAS: defining, designing, building, and reviewing.

When a teacher or group of teachers begins the process of designing an instructional experience for a group of learners, they work sequentially through the four CUTLAS stages. There is a CUTLAS planning document to help them do this; it is divided into the four CUTLAS stages and represents the master plan or strategy underpinning the design of the instructional experience in question. You can access the planning document via my website at *https://drkevinl.wixsite.com/drkevinlmerry*.

## Defining

First is the defining phase. This is when the teacher focuses on the level of variability in their learners and specifies the aims and purpose of the instructional experience they wish to design. The aim of the defining phase is to begin the process of defining what the instructional experience is about, whom it will be for, and what the broad outcomes of the experience should be. Table 14-2 shows a simplified snippet of the defining stage of the CUTLAS planning document.

**TABLE 14-2.** The CUTLAS Defining Stage

| STAGE 1: DEFINING |
|---|
| Date: _____ |
| Program Title: _____ |
| Unit/Module Title: _____ |
| Topic: _____ |
| **Who is teaching this topic?**<br>[List instructors here] |
| **Learners**<br>Who are your learners? What sources of variability are present in your learners? |
| **Background to the topic**<br>What unit/module and program does this topic belong to? What is the mode of delivery? What level is this topic being delivered to? |

| STAGE 1: DEFINING |
|---|
| **Previous feedback**<br>What have learners said in the past about the teaching of this topic? Areas of strength? Areas that need to be developed? |
| **Collaborators**<br>Are you getting anyone to help you design this instructional experience? Learning technologist, librarian, disability specialist, critical friend, etc.? |

## Designing

Designing is the second stage and consists of two parts. The first part involves creating a blueprint for the instructional design that includes creating the learning outcomes or goals, the evaluation activities, and initial ideas for the learning activities, as well as potential outlets and opportunities for learner feedback. Essentially, the blueprint will include some details on each element of the Roadmap for Teaching. Table 14-3 shows a simplified snippet of the blueprint.

**TABLE 14-3.** The CUTLAS Designing Stage

| STAGE 2: DESIGNING |
|---|
| **Aims and purpose**<br>What are the principal aims and intentions of the instructional experience? What should the learners not miss as part of their learning experience? |
| **What do you want the learners to know or be able to do?**<br>What do you want the learners to know or be able to do as a result of the instructional experience? |

| STAGE 2: DESIGNING |
|---|
| **Learning outcomes**<br>Create 2-4 learning outcomes that reflect the key information in the preceding section. Make sure they are SMART, challenging, and pitched at the appropriate academic level. |
| **Evaluation activities**<br>How do you intend to evaluate learner achievement of the learning outcomes considering their variability and any subsequent barriers that may arise? |
| **Assessment for and as learning**<br>Will there be opportunities for or clear links to formative assessment? What opportunities will there be for peer assessment and peer feedback? What opportunities will there be for self-assessment and reflection? |
| **Learning activities/constructive alignment**<br>What learning activities will you use and how do they align with the learning outcomes and evaluation activities? How do the learning activities consider learner variability and subsequent barriers that may arise? |
| **Learner feedback**<br>When and how will learners provide feedback on the instructional experience? How will the feedback be used? |

The second part of the designing phase involves the storyboard, where the teacher plots the learner's learning journey—the key elements of the Roadmap for Teaching detailed in their blueprint—through the instructional experience. "Plotting" in this respect means including a visual representation of each key element of the roadmap onto the storyboard. Traditionally, this is done using different colored sticky notes, but you could do this however you wish. The storyboard is where different pathways that lead to the achievement of the learning goals or outcomes are created based on the variability of the learners, as discussed in Chapter 7 and illustrated in Figure 7-1.

The storyboard is the visual plan of the instructional experience being designed, including all the critical elements of the Roadmap for Teaching as well as a few others. The storyboard brings the blueprint to life by helping teachers to discover how it can be delivered in practice. Storyboarding can be the most challenging part of the design process, but it can also be the most fun and most rewarding—where the individual learning pathways that guide learners toward the achievement of learning goals become a reality.

The key purpose of the storyboard is to create pathways that lead to the achievement of the learning goals. The focus is on aligning those pathways with the learning goals, providing clear detail on what learners are required to know, what they should be able to do as a result of their learning, how they will learn it, how they will demonstrate that they have learned it, how they will receive and give feedback, and what resources will support their learning. The UDL principles become vitally important at this point, as multiple means of engagement, representation, and action and expression are used to create distinct learning pathways that reduce or remove barriers to learning based on learner variability. The UDL Guidelines (CAST, 2018) can be used to stimulate ideas in this regard.

Initially the storyboard is divided into the three key phases that represent the Cheese Sandwich, as Figure 14-1 shows.

| Achievement of intended learning outcomes | | |
|---|---|---|
| Pre-time with teachers and peers | Time with teachers and peers | Post-time with teachers and peers |

**FIGURE 14-1.** The three phases of the Cheese Sandwich

### *Learning Goals/Outcomes*

Learning outcomes are plotted at the point in the Cheese Sandwich at which the learning that supports their achievement will be employed. Remember that in the Cheese Sandwich the emphasis is placed on the time learners spend with their teachers and peers to support the development of higher-order thinking skills. Conversely, the lower-order thinking skills are developed during self-directed study time. Thus, learning outcomes that require lower-order thinking skills can be plotted during the self-directed learning that happens both before and after learners learn with direct support from teachers and peers. These are the "slices of bread" in the Cheese Sandwich. Conversely, the point at which learners begin to engage in higher-order thinking is when they need the most support from teachers and peers. Hence, learning outcomes that require higher-order thinking skills can be plotted during the time that is directly supported by teachers and peers—the "cheese" in the sandwich. As discussed throughout, make sure the goals/outcomes are challenging to foster engagement. Refer back to Chapter 9 for guidance on setting learning goals or outcomes.

## Evaluation Activities

Next, you'll plot the evaluation activities that demonstrate whether the learners have achieved the learning outcomes. Again, these are plotted at whichever point you intend for learners to demonstrate that they have achieved the outcomes. For example, just because the learning that supports achievement of a learning outcome happens in, say, the "pre–time with teachers and peers" phase, it doesn't mean that the evaluation activity must take place then as well. It might be the case that the evaluation activity takes place during the "post–time with teachers and peers" phase. How you structure this aspect is up to you. The key is that you include evaluation activities as part of your plan and that they align directly with the learning outcomes. As discussed in Chapter 11, evaluation activities should include variety and an element of learner choice. There should be opportunities for learners to evaluate themselves and others, and the focus should be on mastery-oriented feedback, which is a core part of assessment *as* learning—a process that supports learners to develop effective learning habits and strategies on their way to becoming expert learners as per the aims of UDL. Mastery-oriented feedback is covered in more detail in Chapter 12. Refer back to Chapter 11 for guidance on setting evaluation activities.

## Learning Activities

After plotting evaluation activities, you'll plot the learning activities. These activities constitute the learning that supports achievement of learning outcomes, so they should be scheduled alongside those learning outcomes. For example, if you intend for your learners to engage in learning that supports achievement of a given learning outcome during the "time with teachers and peers" phase of the Cheese Sandwich, then you should schedule the learning activities that support achievement of that outcome at the same time. Plotting learning activities is an incredibly important part of the CUTLAS process because this is where you articulate what learners will be *doing* to achieve the learning outcomes. The word *doing* is emphasized to reflect that learning opportunities for learners should be active and collaborative. Remember from Chapter 10 that learning activities should align directly with learning outcomes. They should enable active practice of the skills articulated in the learning outcomes, and they should be challenging, fun, interesting, enjoyable, and varied to support learner engagement. Finally, learning activities should provide an outlet for feedback and lead directly to and reflect evaluation activities. Indeed, the learning outcomes, learning activities, and evaluation activities in your storyboard should all be aligned as encouraged in the blueprint seen in Table 14-3. Refer back to Chapter 10 for guidance on setting learning activities.

### Teacher Activities

Another critical activity to plot during the storyboarding phase is the teacher activities. What will you be doing to support your learners to learn effectively? An obvious teacher activity will be to provide feedback to learners when they engage in learning activities and again when they engage in evaluation activities as per the Roadmap for Teaching. Other important teacher activities may include the parts of the EDUCARE? mnemonic, covered in Chapter 10, that you will be responsible for. For example, as part of the teaching of a skill, be it cognitive or practical, will you be explaining the skill and its importance? Will you be demonstrating the skill? As mentioned above, you will be providing a "check and correct" service through feedback when learners are engaging in the practice and evaluation of the skill. When will you be responding to learner questions? Include such considerations in your storyboard.

### Resources

Finally, you'll plot the resources you require to support learning in your learners. For example, will you require your learners to use handouts, quizzes, tasks, or other materials on the learning management system (LMS) as part of their learning experience? Online learning resources may be very important to the self-directed learning that the learners are required to engage in. Will your learners require paper, sticky notes, pens, crayons, and other supplies to be able to engage in the learning activities you've set for them? It can be useful to consider the resources required for each aspect that you plot on the storyboard. For example, will you require some presentation slides, handouts, or a poster displaying the learning outcomes? What will the learners need to successfully engage in learning activities? What will you require to engage in teacher activities? What resources will be required for the delivery of feedback and the evaluation of learning? As above, it can be useful to consider EDUCARE? when thinking about resources. You may provide a video, handout, or podcast to help explain a skill. You may provide a physical demonstration as well as a supplementary video. How will you provide an aide memoir for the skill? Whatever resources you will need, you should plot them on your storyboard at the point at which they will be needed. Be sure that you strictly adhere to the UDL principle of representation when considering learning resources, based on the variability of your learners. Refer back to Chapter 2 for guidance on the representation principle.

Learning outcomes have traditionally been represented by orange sticky notes, evaluation activities by yellow sticky notes, learning activities by green sticky notes, teacher activities by blue sticky notes, and resources by pink sticky notes. Once complete, your storyboard will be a colorful representation of the plan of your instructional experience. Figure 14-2 shows a mock example (albeit in shades of gray).

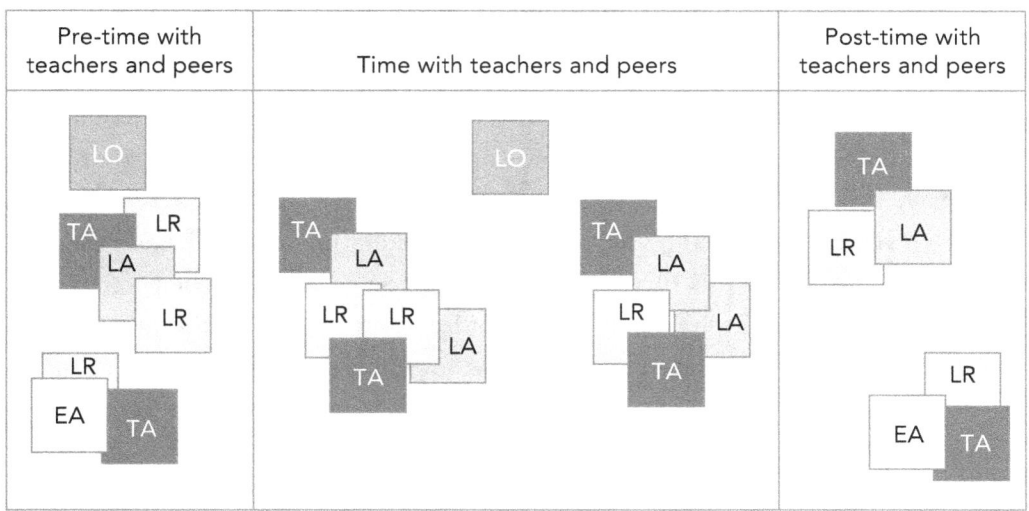

**FIGURE 14-2.** Mock-up of a CUTLAS storyboard

Although this is a hypothetical example included for illustrative purposes, Figure 14-2 shows how the critical design elements can be plotted using CUTLAS. You can see that there is a learning outcome (LO) plotted in the "pre–time with teachers and peers" phase of the Cheese Sandwich. We would expect this to be an outcome that encompasses lower-order thinking skills because the learning that supports the achievement of lower-order skills can be undertaken during self-directed learning. Accompanying the learning outcome in this phase is an evaluation activity (EA) to evaluate whether the corresponding learning outcome has been achieved, a learning activity (LA) to support practice of the skills articulated in the learning outcome, and some accompanying learning resources (LR). The resources support the first teacher activity (TA), which would likely encompass a brief of some sort explaining the learning activity and which also represents a teacher activity. The other teacher activity is linked to the evaluation activity and represents feedback on the evaluation activity. There is also a resource linked here because the feedback would likely be delivered through the LMS.

Next, you can see a second learning outcome plotted in the "time with teachers and peers" phase of the Cheese Sandwich. We would expect this outcome to encompass higher-order thinking skills because mastery of these skills requires support from teachers and peers. There are several learning activities, some of which may represent learners giving feedback to each other following engagement with other learning activities. There are also accompanying resources and teacher activities which would represent elements of the EDUCARE? mnemonic (Petty, 2014), such as explaining, demonstrating, checking and correcting through feedback, and answering learner questions. The evaluation activity for the second learning outcome happens during the "post–time with teachers and peers" phase. This is accompanied by a teacher activity (which could be feedback on the evaluation activity) and a resource (which could be an explanation of the evaluation activity). There is a further learner activity in this phase too, with an accompanying teacher activity and resource. This might involve the revisiting of learning covered in the previous two phases. Regardless of the details, Figure 14-2 shows how the critical design elements can be plotted onto the storyboard. Figure 14-3 shows a photo of a real storyboard created for a three-day Introduction to Teaching in Higher Education course for novice teachers. The photo shows the storyboard for the first day of the course. Notice the adoption of the Cheese Sandwich approach, and the variety of learner activities, learning resources, and evaluation activities, reflecting multiple means of engagement, representation, and action and expression. Also notice the learning outcomes and teacher activities.

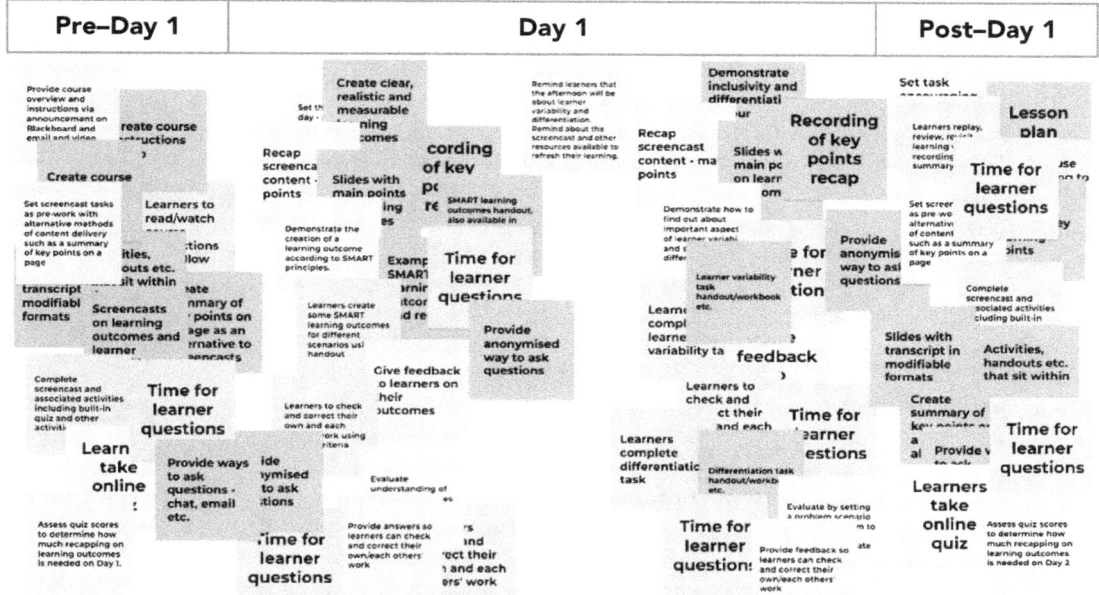

**FIGURE 14-3.** Photo of a real CUTLAS storyboard

## Building

Stage 3 is the building phase, where the learning activities, evaluation activities, and resources designed in stage 2 are actually created if they do not already exist. Due to the flipped learning elements of the Cheese Sandwich and the active, blended focus, teachers are encouraged to build at least some of their activities and resources directly into the LMS. For example, the activities and resources that support self-directed learning would almost certainly be built into the LMS. As mentioned in Chapter 7, the use of multimedia technologies such as screencasts, videos, and podcasts is encouraged as a means of content engagement. It is expected that these multimedia elements would be embedded into the LMS. Table 14-4 shows a simplified snippet of the building stage of the CUTLAS planning document.

**TABLE 14-4.** The CUTLAS Building Stage

| STAGE 3: BUILDING |
|---|
| **Learning activities (repeat for each one)**<br>Activity (what is the activity?):<br><br>Task (what do the learners have to do?):<br><br>Purpose (how is the activity supporting learning/achievement of learning goals?):<br><br>Reflections/feedback (how do you feel about the activity?): |
| **Evaluation activities (repeat for each one)**<br>Activity (what is the activity?):<br><br>Task (what do the learners have to do?):<br><br>Purpose (how is the activity supporting learning/achievement of learning goals?):<br><br>Reflections/feedback (how do you feel about the activity?): |
| **Resources (repeat for each one)**<br>Resource (what is the resource?):<br><br>Use (what do the learners have to do with it?):<br><br>Purpose (how is the resource supporting learning/achievement of learning goals?):<br><br>Reflections/feedback (how do you feel about the resource?): |

## Reviewing

Stage 4 is the reviewing stage, during which the plan for the instructional experience—including learning outcomes, learning activities, evaluation activities, resources, and outlets for feedback (to and from learners)—is reviewed and given feedback. This is usually done by a small team of colleagues and, of course, learners. Whatever the source, feedback on the planned instructional experience is essential for quality assurance, providing the driver for any necessary modifications you may make to the instructional design. The reviewing stage is vital to the quality of your design, such that you can make modifications and improvements before you have even implemented it with your learners. Table 14-5 shows a simplified snippet of the reviewing part of the CUTLAS planning document.

**TABLE 14-5.** The CUTLAS Reviewing Stage

| STAGE 4: REVIEWING |
|---|
| **Learning goals/outcomes**<br>Is it clear what the learners will know or be able to do as a result of the instructional experience? Are the goals and outcomes SMART and challenging? |
| **Learning activities**<br>Are the activities aligned to the learning goals? Is it clear what learners are required to do? Are the activities easy to follow? Is there sufficient variety to meet variable learning needs? What are the good and useful aspects? What could be improved? |
| **Evaluation activities**<br>Are the activities aligned to the learning goals? Is it clear what learners are required to do? Are the evaluation activities easy to follow? Is there sufficient variety to meet variable learning needs? Are there opportunities for self and peer evaluation? What are the good and useful aspects? What could be improved? |

*(continued)*

**TABLE 14-5.** The CUTLAS Reviewing Stage *(continued)*

| STAGE 4: REVIEWING |
| --- |
| **Feedback**<br>Is there feedback planned when learners undertake learning activities? Is there feedback planned when learners undertake evaluation activities? Are there opportunities for learner reflection on their learning? Are there opportunities for learners to give feedback to each other? Are there opportunities for learners to provide feedback to the teacher? |
| **Teacher activities**<br>Do the teacher activities support the aims and purpose of the experience and support achievement of learning goals and outcomes? Is feedback included as a teacher activity? Is the teacher taking the time to explain, demonstrate, and remind learners about important learning points and skills? |
| **Resources**<br>Is it clear how the resources support learning? Are the resources clear and easy to follow? Is there sufficient variety to meet variable learning needs? What are the good and useful aspects? What could be improved? |
| **Overall impressions**<br>What are the strengths of this learning design? What could be improved? |

CUTLAS aims to support the firm embedding of each ingredient required to support mastery over learning as part of the instructional design process. In addition, CUTLAS safeguards the constructive alignment of instructional experiences, ensuring that intended learning outcomes, learning and teaching activities, and evaluation activities are all clearly aligned.

**ACTIVITY** Using the information and tools contained in this chapter, try creating an instructional experience using the CUTLAS approach.

# 15

# Evaluating Learning and Teaching

Teaching is far from a simple endeavor, and it's unlikely that you'll ever feel like you've figured it all out. Instead, you'll probably continue to develop your understanding of how to teach effectively throughout your career, adapting and modifying how you teach to meet ever-changing demands.

Teaching constantly changes. All the time, we are required to discover new skills, techniques, technology, ideas, and approaches that test us and demand that we "up our game," move with the times, and meet new challenges head-on. Teaching never stands still, and so you must never stand still, taking a proactive approach to developing your practice. Incidentally, teaching's ever-changing nature is precisely why it's such a fascinating and rewarding journey. Think of it like this: If you're not improving, you're getting worse. The picture changes so quickly in education. Methods that worked well a decade ago may not work so well with today's learners, given their different expectations, especially around the use of technology. Improvement has to be continual to keep pace with those changes.

It is helpful to remember that teaching is a learnable skill, which means you can get better with deliberate, intentional practice and improvement. The deliberate and intentional part is important. Few people who ever improved at anything did so by accident. The starting point for deliberate and intentional improvement is to focus on the skills that you have yet to master as a teacher—those that you could do better for the benefit of supporting effective learning in your learners. It's often tempting to blame poor instructional experiences on the learners, the time of day, the location, the equipment or facilities, and so on. Each of these factors is often beyond the teacher's control and thus makes a convenient excuse for poor teaching. In contrast, the effective teacher makes a deliberate point of focusing on what can be controlled as part of an instructional experience, the things that they can influence to increase the quality of the learning experience. Chief among these controllable factors is teaching capability—that is, the knowledge, skills, behaviors, and abilities associated with effective teaching. This is one factor that the teacher is solely responsible for. Effective teachers are always trying to improve, changing their practice, trying new things, and action planning, because they are continually learning how to become better teachers.

# EVALUATION

Do you know which teaching skills you haven't mastered? Are you aware of the skills that you could or should improve? How do you know your teaching has been impactful in terms of supporting effective learning? These are important questions to ask yourself when starting the journey of deliberate and intentional improvement. The first step in becoming aware of the skills you could improve upon is to evaluate your teaching—in other words, to judge how effective it is in supporting learners to achieve learning goals. Evaluation is about the ways you gather feedback on your learning, teaching, assessment, and feedback practices in terms of how well you support learners to meet intended learning goals. Remember, part of your role and responsibility as a teacher is to ensure the effectiveness of your teaching in relation to learners developing their learning. It's likely that the quality regulations in the institution where you work will expect you to continually enhance the learning experience of your learners. You cannot do this effectively without evaluation.

> **PAUSE AND THINK** Without thinking too long or too hard, which teaching skills do you need to develop to improve your practice?

## Sources of Information and Data for Evaluation

You have several sources of evidence and data at your disposal for ongoing evaluation of your teaching. You can use both formal and informal approaches to gather triangulated information and data about the impact of your teaching on supporting learning. You can then use this evidence to develop and enhance your teaching practice. Some important sources may include the following:

- Learner performance in evaluation activities and formative/summative assessment
- Learner feedback on their learning experience
- Feedback from peer-supported review or observation activities
- Personal structured reflections on practice
- Information derived from internal or external evaluation and review activities
- The extent to which your teaching reflects formal quality requirements as detailed in institutional and professional or national frameworks

An obvious source of information on your teaching is learner feedback, but you may also get feedback from peers and other evaluative processes, such as unit or module evaluation or external review activities. It is important to note that broader evaluative processes including external activities may not be specifically and directly about your teaching. It's unlikely that you personally will be the focus of such activities. Instead, judgments will likely be made about the overall quality of education in the program you teach or at the institution where you work, but nevertheless, there may be general information resulting from such activities that you can use as feedback and a driver to enhance your teaching.

It is likely that there will be standard institutional mechanisms to obtain feedback from learners on their learning experience and the quality of the teaching they receive within the institution where you work. These are not enough. You must go beyond simply relying on these standard processes and regularly obtain feedback from your learners. Ideally, this should happen each time they engage in an instructional experience. For example, most unit/program evaluations happen at the end of the unit or program they are attached to. By this point, the feedback is too late to effect any changes to your teaching approach for the learners in question. Some possible ways to obtain ongoing feedback include the following:

- Paper or online surveys completed at several points in the semester or year
- Session-by-session exit ticket feedback: What went well? What could be better?

- In-session sticky note feedback: What went well? What could be better?
- Weekly online feedback or chat forums
- Mid- and end-of-semester, or year, focus groups
- Regular check-in with unit/program representatives
- Mid- and end-of-year teacher-learner learning committees
- Learner self-evaluation of progress completed at several points in the semester or year

This list is not exhaustive, and you may be able to come up with your own ideas. However, the key point here is that there are multiple ways to get continual feedback on your teaching from learners that go above and beyond the standardized unit/program evaluations you'll likely be required to undertake.

## UDL-Specific Questionnaire

In their journal article "Universal Design for Learning: Learner and Faculty Perceptions," Lynne Kennette and Nathan Wilson (2019) created a UDL learner perception survey (Table 15-1), part of which measures the extent to which learners experience UDL-related teaching approaches in their learning experiences. The survey consists of 36 items adapted from the list of CAST (2018) UDL checkpoints for each of the three UDL principles. Responses to each dimension follow a five-point Likert scale (1–5) where 1 = Never; 2 = Rarely; 3 = Sometimes; 4 = Often; and 5 = Always. Since the survey items reflect the CAST UDL checkpoints, each of which is supported with empirical evidence, the survey is considered high in *face validity*, and therefore is a quick and easy way to evaluate the extent to which you are applying UDL practices in your teaching.

**TABLE 15-1.** UDL Learner Perception Survey (Adapted From Kennette and Wilson, 2019)

| | FOR EACH ITEM, INDICATE HOW MUCH YOU HAVE EXPERIENCED THIS IN YOUR COURSE. HOW MUCH DID YOUR TEACHER: | NEVER 1 | RARELY 2 | SOMETIMES 3 | OFTEN 4 | ALWAYS 5 |
|---|---|---|---|---|---|---|
| 1 | Present the same course content in multiple ways (video, text, images, etc.) | | | | | |

| FOR EACH ITEM, INDICATE HOW MUCH YOU HAVE EXPERIENCED THIS IN YOUR COURSE. HOW MUCH DID YOUR TEACHER: | | NEVER 1 | RARELY 2 | SOMETIMES 3 | OFTEN 4 | ALWAYS 5 |
|---|---|---|---|---|---|---|
| 2 | Offer electronic versions of textbooks | | | | | |
| 3 | Post handouts online (or make them available digitally) | | | | | |
| 4 | Include subtitles on videos (closed captioned) | | | | | |
| 5 | Upload files that can be read using text-to-speech software (e.g., Word documents, PDFs) | | | | | |
| 6 | Provide clear guidelines for summative (graded) assessments (e.g., example/sample assessment) | | | | | |
| 7 | Include a field trip | | | | | |
| 8 | Capture teaching sessions and make them available to stream before or after class (video or podcast) | | | | | |
| 9 | Make available a glossary of terms (online or other) | | | | | |
| 10 | Offer alternatives for auditory info (e.g., transcripts of videos) and visual info (e.g., description of images) | | | | | |
| 11 | Highlight patterns and relationships in the course content | | | | | |
| 12 | Offer interesting and relevant summative (graded) assessments | | | | | |
| 13 | Allow for some autonomy and/or control in learner learning (e.g., options for practice) and graded assessments (topic and/or format); or choices on tests (choose 1 of 2 essay questions; or pick 5 of the following terms to define) | | | | | |

*(continued)*

**TABLE 15-1.** UDL Learner Perception Survey (Adapted From Kennette and Wilson, 2019) *(continued)*

| | FOR EACH ITEM, INDICATE HOW MUCH YOU HAVE EXPERIENCED THIS IN YOUR COURSE. HOW MUCH DID YOUR TEACHER: | NEVER 1 | RARELY 2 | SOMETIMES 3 | OFTEN 4 | ALWAYS 5 |
|---|---|---|---|---|---|---|
| 14 | Provide clear guidelines for summative (graded) assessments (e.g., example/sample assignment) | | | | | |
| 15 | Let learners decide which topics are covered in the course | | | | | |
| 16 | Use hands-on activities in class | | | | | |
| 17 | Connect course content to real-world experiences | | | | | |
| 18 | Communicate with learners (in class, outside of class, online, or via email) | | | | | |
| 19 | Provide clear and specific feedback on assessments | | | | | |
| 20 | Offer a choice of how learners want to receive feedback on assessments (e.g., verbal or written feedback) | | | | | |
| 21 | Allow learners to resubmit assessments | | | | | |
| 22 | Include peer evaluation as part of the course or assessments | | | | | |
| 23 | Make PowerPoint slides available to learners | | | | | |
| 24 | Include group work and collaboration with other learners (e.g., discussions) | | | | | |
| 25 | Provide opportunities for self-assessment/self-evaluation and reflection | | | | | |

| FOR EACH ITEM, INDICATE HOW MUCH YOU HAVE EXPERIENCED THIS IN YOUR COURSE. HOW MUCH DID YOUR TEACHER: | | NEVER 1 | RARELY 2 | SOMETIMES 3 | OFTEN 4 | ALWAYS 5 |
|---|---|---|---|---|---|---|
| 26 | Answer questions about course content or assessments outside of class (e.g., online, via email) | | | | | |
| 27 | Use gender-neutral language and inclusive examples (race/culture, etc.) | | | | | |
| 28 | Minimize threats and distractions in the learning environment | | | | | |
| 29 | Motivate learners to do their best work | | | | | |
| 30 | Offer flexible due dates on summative (graded) assessments (e.g., allowed to submit it late) | | | | | |
| 31 | Offer formative (practice/ungraded) assessments to practice the course content | | | | | |
| 32 | Provide sufficient (or unlimited) time for tests | | | | | |
| 33 | Provide rubrics for summative (graded) assessments | | | | | |
| 34 | Guide you in using increasingly difficult activities or formative (practice/ungraded) and summative (graded) assessments | | | | | |
| 35 | Guide goal setting and the development of learner learning strategies | | | | | |
| 36 | Provide opportunities for learners to monitor progress (e.g., grades posted online, regular in-session feedback) | | | | | |

## Peer-Supported Review

Observation of teaching has long been considered an integral part of teacher development in higher education (Gosling & O'Connor, 2009), providing teachers with a situated learning opportunity to develop experientially through reflection upon practice (Becher, 1999; Knight, Tait, & Yorke, 2006; Kolb, 1984; Lave & Wenger, 1991; Mintzberg, 2004).

There are several different approaches to teacher observation—too numerous to mention here, though many include third-party, hierarchical observation elements. Such models are characterized by summative judgments of teaching via grading systems, and the sharing of observation information with superiors such as line managers (Gosling, 2002; McMahon, Barrett, & O'Neill, 2007). They are used primarily for performance management, auditing, appraisal, probation, promotion, quality assurance, accountability, and authentication of practice (Gosling, 2002; McMahon et al., 2007). Frequently, due to their judgmental nature, such schemes are perceived negatively by teachers, risking alienation, lack of engagement, and sometimes outright opposition (Gosling, 2002; McMahon et al., 2007).

A further limitation of teaching observation schemes is that feedback is provided to teachers only on the aspects of teaching and learning that take place in the classroom. This is just one part of the learner learning journey. Furthermore, classroom observations tend to focus on the performance aspects of teaching at the expense of other important learning experiences (Gosling & O'Connor, 2009).

A potential solution to these limitations is *Peer-Supported Review (P-SR)* (Gosling & O'Connor, 2009; Gosling, 2014), a method of developing teaching and supporting learning practice through peer-to-peer discussion and self-reflection (Gosling & O'Connor, 2009). P-SR offers a more flexible approach to the peer review of teaching than observation alone, since it allows the supported review of any topic relating to learning (Gosling & O'Connor, 2009). Hence, it's far better suited to evaluating UDL learning, teaching, and assessment practices, which should encompass the three principles of engagement, representation, and action and expression. Critically, P-SR is a nonjudgmental process, based on shared dialogue. Colleagues are safe to reflect on practice, generating a collaborative learning opportunity. There are no grades with P-SR, since when a grade is given, we tend to focus more on it (just like our learners!) than on the most important element: the feedback we receive.

As a general rule, a P-SR scheme covers three important elements:

- Peer observation of teaching
- Peer-supported enhancement of a specific area of practice
- Peer-supported learner review

As you can see, the review of practice goes beyond what happens in the classroom. Since UDL is about enabling greater choice and learner control over learning, P-SR embraces such values. Within each of these elements, teachers are given control over how the process of P-SR unfolds, meaning that the feedback and subsequent learning that results from P-SR is directed and determined by the teacher engaged in the learning. Thus, P-SR is a highly personalized means of evaluating and improving teaching practice. As you've read throughout this book, when learning is personalized, it has greater meaning to the individual, enhancing interest and engagement.

You may already be required to engage in some sort of peer observation or review process as part of your institution's or context's current evaluative processes. However, if you have the opportunity to engage in P-SR or if you're interested in trying it, it's important to ensure you have the choice of or control over several critical elements of the process, as detailed by McMahon et al. (2007):

- The observer/reviewer
- The focus of the review
- How feedback is provided
- Information arising from observation/review
- What's done as a result of the review

In terms of who reviews your learning, teaching, assessment, and feedback practices, this can be any peer who you nominate since P-SR is about gaining support from and providing support to peers. However, to maximize the quality of feedback and subsequent learning and enhancement from P-SR, it is perhaps best to be reviewed by a teacher who has substantial learning and teaching expertise or experience as well as a working knowledge and understanding of UDL.

## Peer Observation of Teaching

For the peer observation of teaching element, teachers work in partnership with a reviewer to gain feedback on and ultimately enhance their classroom-based teaching practices. As part of this process, the teacher provides a detailed briefing on the teaching session to be observed, including information about the learners, the learning goals, and the demonstration of UDL teaching practices that will be utilized throughout the instructional experience. The reviewer observes the instructional experience, paying close attention to the extent to which UDL is espoused in the teacher's practice and the extent to which learning takes place for the learners. The reviewer then provides nonjudgmental feedback.

Following the observation and the delivery of feedback to the teacher, the teacher and observer together discuss how the learning experience could be further improved. They collaboratively draw up an action plan, which contains clear goals, targets, and dates for development and acts as a learning contract for further development. Once the plan is finalized and shared with the reviewer, the teacher works toward their targets, which may involve repeating the observation process or engaging in the other elements of P-SR. The teacher produces a report on what they achieved as a result of the observation and action plan. The teacher can decide if and how they want this to be shared with colleagues as a supportive resource.

## Peer-Supported Enhancement of a Specific Area of Practice

For the peer-supported enhancement of a specific area of practice, the teacher works collaboratively with a peer reviewer to gain feedback on and ultimately enhance a specific area of learning, teaching, assessment, and feedback practice. This will typically involve non-classroom-based learning and teaching practices, though the process may require a reviewer to observe one of the teacher's instructional experiences. Any area of teaching practice can be reviewed, but typical examples include feedback on the suitability of assessment methods, how well learner feedback is provided, the quality and accessibility of learning resources, and how well learning activities and evaluation activities support achievement of learning goals. The process may involve visiting and/or reviewing the teacher's LMS, session plans, learning and teaching resources, and the like. As with the peer observation of teaching element, the reviewer provides nonjudgmental feedback and collaborates with the teacher on an action plan. As previously, the action plan contains goals, targets, and dates for the teacher to work toward as part of their ongoing development. The teacher should document what they have learned or achieved throughout the review and action plan process, and then choose whether to share it as a supportive resource for colleagues.

## *Peer-Supported Learner Review*

Not all P-SR schemes have a learner review element, though it can be a very useful source of feedback. With peer-supported learner review, teachers work in partnership with a reviewer and with one or two learners who typically aren't studying the unit, module, or program under consideration. The purpose of peer-supported learner review is to use learner feedback to help teachers reflect on practice through open dialogue about strengths and areas of development. The teacher should have an idea about which learner(s) will participate in the review process, and ideally, should be able to choose them. However, if the teacher has difficulties identifying suitable learners, the reviewer can support this process.

Supported by the reviewer, the learner(s) review aspects of the teacher's learning, teaching, assessment, and feedback practices. These aspects may include large- and small-group teaching sessions; the LMS; an assessment brief or instructions; or other documentation, such as a unit/module or program handbook or learning and teaching resources. Before each review, the teacher, reviewer, and learner(s) discuss the context, aim, and focus of the review. The learner(s) take notes during the review process to support their recollections of it. The reviewer supports the learners in the review process by encouraging their reflection on each review. As with the previous two elements, the learners, supported by the reviewer, provide nonjudgmental feedback and help draw up an action plan based on the feedback. As previously, the action plan contains goals, targets, and dates for the teacher to work toward as part of their ongoing development, and the teacher should document, and potentially share with colleagues, their learning and achievements from the process.

Whatever sources of feedback we use as part of our evaluations, we must ensure that we are open-minded and willing to accept constructive criticism of our practice openly, honestly, and gratefully. Feedback is one of the greatest gifts you will ever receive as a teacher, as it contains the seeds of improvement in your practice. However, if your mindset when receiving feedback is closed and defensive, you may fail to gain all of the treasures it contains.

**PAUSE AND THINK** What sources of data and information do you currently use to gain insight into your teaching strengths and areas for development?

## STRUCTURED SELF-REFLECTION

Self-reflection is a prerequisite skill of the effective teacher and represents an important aspect of self-evaluation. The ability to reflect upon your teaching and instructional experiences and learn from them is essential to improvement. Your ability to self-evaluate will largely determine your capacity to improve your teaching. Self-reflection should happen every time you engage in an instructional experience with learners, irrespective of whether you are teaching a large group or engaging in a one-on-one tutorial. Oftentimes, one of the most effective ways to reflect on your practice is to discuss your teaching with your colleagues, making notes on any feedback or ideas you receive. In this regard, it is useful to keep a journal on your teaching where you can jot down your reflections as well as feedback and ideas.

Discussing your teaching with experienced teachers, particularly experienced UDL practitioners, is a prerequisite for developing effective practice, especially if you are facing challenges or wish to address recurring problems. Always be willing to ask more experienced colleagues for advice about problems or challenges you face. It is also useful to perform the various P-SR elements on a more experienced colleague, such as observing their teaching, since you may see how they deal with similar problems and challenges.

Perhaps the easiest and most effective way to self-evaluate using self-reflection is to use a structured reflective process or cycle. Since teaching is an experiential endeavor and many teachers reflect on experience as a means of improvement, the Experiential Learning Cycle by David Kolb is a useful starting point (Kolb, 1984). The Experiential Learning Cycle, at its core, is built on the view that learning is based on experience. It has been used for several decades by many teachers as a means of developing practice through reflections on experience.

Experience is a central facet of learning, but only if it is paired with reflection and related to our theoretical understanding of a given topic. We must then plan how we can improve and put that plan into action. Once we've done so, we must reflect on it some more as part of a repeated, cyclical, and theoretically infinite process (see Figure 15-1). This is essentially experiential learning, and it can be useful when learning anything, not only how to teach more effectively. Working our way through the cycle will enable us to optimize the learning we get from experience, which on its own won't necessarily ensure that anything is learned effectively.

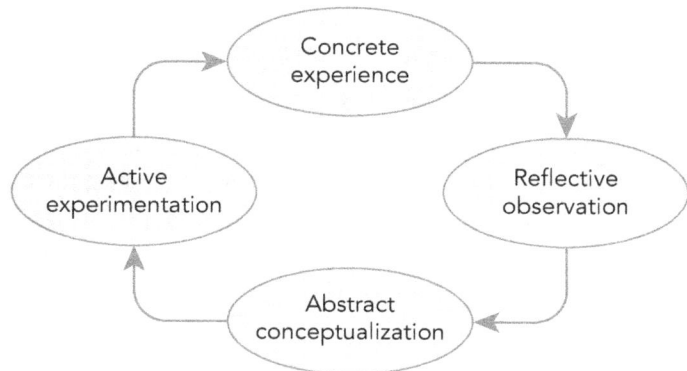

**FIGURE 15-1.** The Experiential Learning Cycle. Adapted from Kolb (1984).

## Concrete Experience

Concrete experience means actually doing or engaging in an activity in a real-world context. An obvious form of concrete experience would be to actually do some teaching. We might call this *direct* concrete experience. However, concrete experience could also happen if you were doing a teaching simulation, such as a microteach, or observing a colleague's practice. We might call this *indirect* concrete experience. As a rule, direct concrete experience tends to be more effective than indirect. Such is the nature of higher education teaching, especially in the UK, that you are usually thrown in at the deep end and required to teach for real without first having the opportunity to participate in a simulation or deliberately observe another's practice to learn to teach. Concrete experience should be used to experiment, try things out, and use new ideas. As part of the cycle, it is influenced directly by active experimentation.

## Reflective Observation

Reflective observation is about reflecting on performance within the activity or experience, considering things that went well and things that could be improved. Reflection can be aided by the feedback you gather on each session you teach or each of your concrete experiences. In fact, it is critical to use learner feedback to help you reflect, especially if you are new to teaching. I remember the first half-dozen or so teaching sessions I ever delivered, which were large lectures to ~200 learners. I covered all of the required content, on time, and received barely any questions from any of the learners. I even told a few jokes that got a laugh. I went away from those experiences believing I had done a good job. I did not ask for any feedback. However, when I look back on those experiences, I can now see all the mistakes I made and can see that the sessions I delivered were less than ideal. If I had been asked to reflect upon them in my inexperienced state, my reflections might have been that everything was good and that I didn't need to change much. Feedback from the learners would have given me a much more accurate and objective view as to how the sessions really went—what the learners found helpful, what they found less so, what I could do to improve the sessions, and so on.

## Abstract Conceptualization

Abstract conceptualization is about what you've learned from reflections on the activity or experience, including the factors accounting for things that went well or could be improved. Abstract conceptualization is about aligning concrete experience to theory. For example, why did the things that went well go well? Why did the things that went badly go badly? How should various tasks and activities be done in theoretical terms? Why should they be done that way? Did my practice reflect theoretical ideas or were those ideas disregarded? Sometimes concrete experience may confirm whatever the theories say about given issues, and thus abstract conceptualization can be a quick and relatively painless part of the cycle.

## Active Experimentation

Active experimentation is where you consider your reflections on experience and use them to guide your subsequent actions and modifications to your practice or approach. Essentially the teacher asks themselves, "How can I improve in my next teaching session?" There is then an opportunity to try new things in the next teaching session or concrete experience. Active experimentation requires some bravery. It's always tempting to fall back into approaches and methods we're comfortable with. However, you must get out of your comfort zone and try things that are unfamiliar to you. It is useful to write down the specific things you want to try. It is also useful to remember that if you make mistakes, it's okay—it's all part of the learning experience. Sometimes it pays to be open and honest with your learners by telling them that you'll be trying some new things based on their feedback and that you can see how it goes together. This way, you won't feel as bad if you make mistakes and the learners will value that you've used their feedback in this way.

Here's a really basic teaching example of the cycle in action:

**Concrete Experience**   Teacher delivers a teaching session to a group of learners.

**Reflective Observation**   Teacher considers their own performance and feels that they could have got the learners to engage in the session more effectively.

**Abstract Conceptualization**   Teacher feels that learners did not engage as effectively as possible because there were limited types of learning activities.

**Active Experimentation**   Teacher actively plans a variety of learning activities as a means of improving engagement in subsequent teaching sessions.

Each stage in the cycle is critical, especially the active experimentation phase. You must try new things continually to develop your practice. Don't worry if you have the odd disaster when trying new things. In fact, you should expect that there will be mistakes and challenges. This isn't a problem. In fact, if you rarely make mistakes or experience challenges and failures, you're probably not experimenting enough.

We can access the Experiential Learning Cycle at any point, but it's important that we follow the sequence of the cycle and not skip any points. One thing I've always liked about the cycle is that it can help to reframe mistakes and poor performance. Rather than view such things as catastrophic, the Experiential Learning Cycle helps us to view them as important and inevitable experiences to reflect upon, which can be used to support our learning and subsequent improvement.

Here are some important points to remember about evaluating your teaching:

- Make a point of reflecting on each session you teach.

- Remember to think about what went well and what did not go well.

- Try to unpack your teaching by asking *why* things went well or not so well.

- Try to come up with clear action steps or things to try in your next session.

- Apply action steps gained from one session to the next session you teach.
- Make a point of discussing your teaching with colleagues or a mentor.
- Get feedback from your learners following every session you teach.
- Engage in some aspect of peer-supported review and reflect on the feedback you gain.
- Use the Experiential Learning Cycle as a means of deliberately reflecting on and improving your teaching.

# FEEDBACK

Just like our learners, teachers learn best from informative feedback. As Geoff Petty would say, teachers also require medals telling them what they do well and why they do it well, as well as a mission telling them what and how they need to improve (Petty, 2014). Try to make sure, even if you have to ask for it, that the feedback you receive on your teaching contains these elements where possible. While it wouldn't be appropriate to ask a learner how you can improve since they may not know, if you've been observed by a more experienced colleague, it's reasonable to ask them for advice on why something was done well or how you can improve.

> **PAUSE AND THINK** Do you currently try to reflect on each of the instructional experiences or teaching sessions you deliver? What sources of information do you use to support those reflections? Do you experiment, modify, or try new approaches based on those reflections? If not, could you begin to do this?

# ACTION PLANNING

A final word on action planning: Evaluation of your teaching is all well and good, but you must then put that evaluative information to use to improve your teaching. This is where action planning becomes critical. As you've probably noticed, action planning features prominently in several of the evaluative processes discussed previously, particularly the various aspects of peer-supported review.

In its most basic sense, an action plan is a strategy that identifies the steps required to achieve a goal. In the context of teaching, the goals are the aspects of your teaching practice you wish to develop. Revisiting the example used earlier in this chapter, you may want to become better at designing a variety of active learning activities to use in teaching sessions. In this scenario, your action plan would consist of the action-oriented steps you will take to get better at designing a wider variety of active learning activities. This is not a comprehensive discussion of action planning processes, nor an exhaustive source of different action planning approaches, but as a general rule an action plan should include the following components:

- A clear goal to be achieved (usually an aspect of your teaching to improve)
- Steps you will take to achieve your goal
- A timeframe for when the steps will be completed (milestones and deadlines)
- Support and/or resources needed to complete the tasks
- A way of measuring progress

The following steps will assist you in action planning:

1. **Define clear goals.**

    As mentioned, the goals will be the aspects of your teaching practice you wish to improve. It is useful if your goals adhere to SMART criteria, ensuring they are:

    | | |
    |---|---|
    | **Specific** | Are clearly defined |
    | **Measurable** | Include a way of tracking progress |
    | **Achievable** | Are attainable for the context (time, resources, experience, etc.) |
    | **Relevant** | Clearly represent identified areas of improvement |
    | **Timely** | Specify a clear end date |

2. **List the steps to be taken.**

    This is where you list the steps you must take to achieve your goal. You can use a grid like Table 15-2 to list the steps, identify required support or resources, and set a deadline for taking each step. It is important to prioritize the steps. For example, using the previous example, you would need to first learn about different types of active learning activities that you could use in your teaching before you started to apply them in practice.

3. **Set milestones and deadlines.**

   Milestones are like mini-goals that support the achievement of the main goal. They help to keep you motivated and committed to your main goal. It is useful to start with the main goal and work backward as you set milestones. For instance, sticking with the previous example, a milestone might be to have three new active learning activities that you will try out in sessions two weeks after you set your main goal. The next milestone may be to have tried out the three activities and received feedback on them from learners two weeks after that.

4. **Identify support and resources.**

   What support will you need to take each of the steps in your action plan? Will you need to talk to a colleague or observe their teaching for ideas, for example? What resources will you need? Do you need a particular book, journal, or other teaching resource? Using the previous example, what resources will you need to find out about different active learning activities that you could use? Will you need a book, website, or blog, or can you just go observe some colleagues?

5. **Visualize your plan.**

   It can be very useful to have a visual representation of your action plan in the form of a GANTT chart, table, flowchart, or calendar. This way, you can closely track your milestones and deadlines, as well as use the visualization as a further source of motivation.

6. **Evaluate progress.**

   Make sure you set aside some time to evaluate how you progress in achieving your goal. The evaluation aspects link to the measurable part of your goal; you must have a way of knowing if it has been successfully achieved. To get better at creating and using a variety of active learning activities, you can easily track your progress by getting feedback from your learners. Better still, you'll be doing this anyway as part of your ongoing evaluation of your teaching.

Table 15-2 shows a possible action plan for the goal of improving at designing a variety of active learning activities. Notice how the plan has a clear goal, with a clear deadline and milestones. The steps are clearly described, and the required support and resources identified. There are several opportunities for evaluation. The plan, particularly the milestones, could easily be added to a calendar or presented in chart form. Each step could even be crossed off or given a particular color once completed. Feel free to adapt the template in Table 15-2 and use it for yourself.

**PAUSE AND THINK** Do you currently set yourself an action plan at the end/start of each year to support your continuing development as a teacher? Is this something you can begin doing if you don't already?

**TABLE 15-2.** Action Plan Template

**Date:** October 2

**Goal:** To become better at designing a variety of active learning activities

**Deadline:** Beginning of December (approximately eight weeks)

| Step | Support/resources | By when? |
| --- | --- | --- |
| • Find out about some new active learning activities that I don't currently use. | • Obtain a copy of the Active Learning Toolkit by Rob Plevin (2017) to help me identify some new active learning activities. | • October 16, 2023 |
| • Select three new active learning activities to adapt to my teaching context. | • Ask my mentor for advice about adapting different activities to my teaching context and get their view on the usefulness of the activities.<br>• Obtain any physical/virtual learning resources I need to deliver the activities (websites, apps, handouts, notes, stationery, etc.). | • October 30, 2023 |

*(continued)*

**TABLE 15-3.** Action Plan Template *(continued)*

**Date:** October 2

**Goal:** To become better at designing a variety of active learning activities

**Deadline:** Beginning of December (approximately eight weeks)

| Step | Support/resources | By when? |
|---|---|---|
| • Try out my three new active learning activities with my learners over a period of two weeks and obtain continual feedback. | • Create a feedback form for learners to evaluate the new active learning activities.<br>• Ask my mentor to provide feedback on the activities and observe a session in which I use the new activities. | • November 13, 2023 |
| • Make any tweaks to my activities based on learner and mentor feedback and try them out again for another two weeks. | • Continue to use my learner feedback form for learners to evaluate the updated learning activities.<br>• Ask my mentor to provide further feedback on the activities, and observe another session in which I use the new activities. | • November 27, 2023 |
| • Collate learner feedback on the updated learning activities and reflect on the whole process of trying to become better at designing a variety of active learning activities. Document what I've learned and next steps. | • Discuss my reflections and possible next steps with my mentor. | • December 1, 2023 |

# Epilogue

I would define mastery as the achievement of comprehensive knowledge, skill, and ability in a given activity or undertaking. Based on this definition, we can safely conclude that mastery of anything is a challenging endeavor. When attempting to master anything, including the application of UDL as part of your teaching practices, you may face setbacks, periods of frustration, stagnation, and even a lack of perceived progress at various points in your journey. Mastery in any domain is something that requires time, patience, and commitment to achieve. In my experience, mastering the UDL teaching practice requires a learner mindset founded on effort, persistence, trial and error, reflection, and a dedication to iteratively enhancing what you do to support effective learning in your learners. It also ultimately requires an unwavering belief in the idea that what you are doing is the right thing to do. Thus, the difficult times are assuaged by a faith in the value and ethos of an approach that views learner variability as a strength rather than a burden, and where there is a clear recognition that there is always more than one way of supporting effective learning.

It is important to remember that by reading this book and showing an interest in accessible, inclusive, and equitable education through UDL, you are taking the first steps to becoming an agent of change, supporting the cultural shift necessary to push educational institutions into becoming systems that intentionally work to remove and reduce barriers, enabling all learners to reach their true potential. You have already begun to support and promote a new way of doing things. You have already begun working toward creating a tipping point beyond which there can be no return to the old ways of doing things. The work you are doing, and will continue to do in the future, has the potential to significantly change higher education forever, and for the better. Subsequently, you're already incredibly powerful and important to the continued proliferation of UDL within and across institutions of higher education. As a

UDL practitioner, you occupy a unique and important position, since the future is in your hands. You have the potential to shape and determine the attitudes and values of the next generation of teachers, by modeling accessible, inclusive, and equitable practices aimed at creating a more equal and just society. By being a role model and inspiring those around you, you're creating a vision for what the future of education should look like. Good luck, and remember to enjoy your UDL journey!

# References

Anderson, L. W., & Krathwohl, D. R. (Eds.). (2001). *A taxonomy for learning, teaching, and assessing: A revision of Bloom's taxonomy of educational objectives.* Boston, MA: Allyn & Bacon.

Armellini, A., & Jones, S. (2008). Carpe Diem: seizing each day to foster change in e-learning design. *Reflecting Education, 4*(1), 17–29.

Ausubel, D. (1978). *Educational psychology: A cognitive view.* New York, NY: Holt, Rinehart & Winston.

Becher, T. (1999). *Professional practices: Commitment and capability in a changing environment.* London, UK: Routledge.

Bergmann, J., & Sams, A. (2012). *Flip your classroom: Reach every learner in every class every day.* Washington, DC: International Society for Technology in Education.

Biggs, J. (2003). Aligning teaching for constructing learning. *Higher Education Academy, 1*(4), 1–4.

Biggs, J., & Tang, C. (2011). *Teaching for quality learning at university.* London, UK: McGraw-Hill Education.

Black, J., & Moore, E. J. (2019). *UDL navigators in higher education: A field guide.* Wakefield, MA: CAST Professional Publishing.

Black, R. D., Weinberg, L. A., & Brodwin, M. G. (2015). Universal Design for Learning and Instruction: Perspectives of students with disabilities in higher education. *Exceptionality Education International, 25*(2), 1–26.

Bloom, B. S., Engelhart, M. D., Furst, E. J., Hill, W. H., & Krathwohl, D. R. (1956). *Handbook I: Cognitive domain.* New York, NY: David McKay.

Bracken, S., & Novak, K. (Eds.). (2019). *Transforming higher education through universal design for learning: An international perspective.* London, UK: Routledge.

Butler, D. L., & Winne, P. H. (1995). Feedback and self-regulated learning: A theoretical synthesis. *Review of Educational Research, 65*(3), 245–81.

Carless, D., Salter, D., Yang, M., & Lam, J. (2011). Developing sustainable feedback practices. *Studies in Higher Education, 36*, 395–407.

Center for Applied Special Technology (CAST). (2018). *Universal Design for Learning Guidelines*, version 2.2. Wakefield, MA: National Center on Universal Design for Learning.

Chita-Tegmark, M., Gravel, J. W., Maria De Lourdes, B. S., Domings, Y., & Rose, D. H. (2012). Using the Universal Design for Learning framework to support culturally diverse learners. *Journal of Education, 192*(1), 17–22.

Davies, P. L., Schelly, C. L., & Spooner, C. L. (2013). Measuring the effectiveness of universal design for learning intervention in postsecondary education. *Journal of Postsecondary Education and Disability, 26*(3), 195–220.

Dexter, D. D., & Hughes, C. A. (2011). Graphic organizers and students with learning disabilities: A meta-analysis. *Learning Disability Quarterly, 34*(1), 51–72.

Dexter, D. D., Park, Y. J., & Hughes, C. A. (2011). A meta-analytic review of graphic organizers and science instruction for adolescents with learning disabilities: Implications for the intermediate and secondary science classroom. *Learning Disabilities Research & Practice, 26*(4), 204–13.

Earl, L. M., & Katz, S. (2006). Rethinking classroom assessment with purpose in mind: Assessment for, as and of learning. Retrieved from *https://www.edu.gov.mb.ca/k12/assess/wncp/full_doc.pdf*

Espasa, A., & Meneses, J. (2010). Analysing feedback processes in an online teaching and learning environment: An exploratory study. *Higher Education, 59*(3), 277–92.

Evans, C. (2013). Making sense of assessment feedback in higher education. *Review of Educational Research, 83*(1), 70–120.

Fleming, N. D., & Mills, C. (1992). Not another inventory, rather a catalyst for reflection. *To Improve the Academy, 11*(1), 137–55.

Fovet, F. (2020). Universal design for learning as a tool for inclusion in the higher education classroom: Tips for the next decade of implementation. *Education Journal, 9*(6), 163–72.

Fovet, F. (2021). Developing an ecological approach to the strategic implementation of UDL in higher education. *Journal of Education and Learning, 10*(4), 27–39.

Freeman, J. B., Rule, N. O., Adams Jr., R. B., & Ambady, N. (2009). Culture shapes a mesolimbic response to signals of dominance and subordination that associates with behavior. *Neuroimage, 47*(1), 353–59.

Gardner, J. (Ed.). (2011). *Assessment and learning*. London, UK: SAGE Publications.

Gosling, D. (2002). Models of peer observation of teaching. *Learning and Teaching Support Network*. Retrieved from https://www.researchgate.net/publication/267687499_Models_of_Peer_Observation_of_Teaching

Gosling, D. (2014). Collaborative peer supported review of teaching. In J. Sachs & M. Parsell (Eds.), *Peer review of learning and teaching in higher education.* (pp. 13–31). Berlin, Germany: Springer Dordrecht.

Gosling, D., & O'Connor, K. M. (2009). *Beyond peer observation of teaching*. London, UK: Staff and Educational Development Association.

Hattie, J. (2012). *Visible learning for teachers: Maximizing impact on learning*. London, UK: Routledge.

Hattie, J., & Gan, M. (2011). Instruction based on feedback. In R. E. Mayer & P. A. Alexander (Eds.), *Handbook of research on learning and instruction* (pp. 263–85). London, UK: Routledge.

Hattie, J., Fisher, D., Frey, N., Gojak, L. M., Moore, S. D., & Mellman, W. (2016). *Visible learning for mathematics, grades K–12: What works best to optimize student learning*. Thousand Oaks, CA: Corwin Press.

Hubble, S., & Bolton, P. (2020). House of Commons Library: Briefing paper: Number 8716, 22 February 2020: *Support for disabled students in higher education in England*. Retrieved from https://researchbriefings.files.parliament.uk/documents/CBP-8716/CBP-8716.pdf

Hussman, P. R., & O'Loughlin, V. D. (2019). Another nail in the coffin for learning styles? Disparities among undergraduate anatomy students' study strategies, class performance, and reported VARK learning styles. *Anatomical Sciences Education, 12*(1), 6–19.

Immordino-Yang, M. H., & Damasio, A. (2007). We feel, therefore we learn: The relevance of affective and social neuroscience to education. *Mind, Brain, and Education, 1*(1), 3–10.

Kampis, D., & Southgate, V. (2020). Altercentric cognition: How others influence our cognitive processing. *Trends in Cognitive Sciences, 24*(11), 945–59.

Kennette, L. N., & Wilson, N. A. (2019). Universal Design for Learning (UDL): Student and faculty perceptions. *Journal of Effective Teaching in Higher Education, 2*(1), 1–26.

Kibble, J. D. (2017). Best practices in summative assessment. *Advances in Physiology Education, 41*, 110–19.

Knight, P. T., & Yorke, M. (2003). Employability and good learning in higher education. *Teaching in Higher Education, 8*(1), 3–16.

Knight, P., Tait, J., and Yorke, M. (2006). The professional learning of teachers in higher education. *Studies in Higher Education, 31*(3), 319–40.

Kolb, D. A. (1984). *Experiential learning.* Englewood Cliffs, NJ: Prentice-Hall.

Lave, J., & Wenger, E. (1991). *Situated learning: Legitimate peripheral participation.* Cambridge, UK: Cambridge University Press.

Lysaght, Z., & O'Leary, M. (2013). An instrument to audit teachers' use of assessment for learning. *Irish Educational Studies, 32*(2), 217–32.

McMahon, T., Barrett, T., & O'Neill, G. (2007). Using observation of teaching to improve quality; finding your way through competing conceptions, confusion of practice and mutually exclusive intentions. *Teaching in Higher Education, 12*(4), 499–511.

Merry, K. L. (2019). Designing curricula with Universal Design for Learning (UDL). *Educational Developments, 20*(3), 10–14.

Merry, K. L. (2021). Adopting Universal Design for Learning: It's just good teaching. *The Ahead Journal, 13*, 1–8.

Merry, K. L. (2023). Embedding universal design into intensive learning experiences. *Journal of Block & Intensive Learning & Teaching,* 1, 17–27.

Meyer, A., Rose, D. H., & Gordon, D. (2014). *Universal Design for Learning: Theory and practice.* Wakefield, MA: CAST Professional Publishing.

Meyer, R. E. (2002). Rote versus meaningful learning. *Theory Into Practice, 41*(4), 226–32.

Mintzberg, H. (2004). *Managers, not MBAs: A hard look at the soft practice of managing and management development.* San Francisco, CA: Berrett-Koehler Publishers.

Nerantzi, C., & Chatzidamianos, G. (2020). Moving to block teaching during the COVID-19 pandemic. *International Journal of Management and Applied Research, 7*(4), 482–95.

The Office of Communications (Ofcom). (2018). *Communications market report 2018.* Retrieved from *https://www.ofcom.org.uk/research-and-data/multi-sector-research/cmr/cmr-2018/interactive*

The Office for Students. (2020). *"Digital poverty" risks leaving students behind.* Retrieved from *https://www.officeforstudents.org.uk/news-blog-and-events/press-and-media/digital-poverty-risks-leaving-students-behind/*

Ontario Ministry of Education. (2013). *Learning for all: A guide to effective assessment and instruction for all students, kindergarten to grade 12.* Toronto: Author.

Pashler, H., McDaniel, M., Rohrer, D., & Bjork, R. (2009). Learning styles: Concepts and evidence. *Psychological Science in the Public Interest, 9*(3), 105–119.

Petty, G. (2014). *Teaching today: A practical guide.* Oxford, UK: Oxford University Press.

Plevin, R. (2017). *The active learning tool kit: Outrageously engaging activities to increase student participation, raise achievement & have your toughest students asking for more.* Penrith, UK: Life Raft Media.

Race, P. (2019). *The lecturer's toolkit: a practical guide to assessment, learning and teaching.* London, UK: Routledge.

Rose, D. H., & Meyer, A. (2002). *Teaching every student in the digital age: Universal Design for Learning.* Alexandria, VA: Association for Supervision and Curriculum Development.

Sadler, D. R. (1989). Formative assessment and the design of instructional systems. *Instructional Science, 18*(2), 119–44.

Sadler, D. R. (2009). Transforming holistic assessment and grading into a vehicle for complex learning. In G. Joughin (Ed.), *Assessment, learning and judgement in higher education* (pp. 1–19). Berlin, Germany: Springer.

Sadler, D. R. (2010). Beyond feedback: Developing student capability in complex appraisal. *Assessment and Evaluation in Higher Education, 35*(5), 535–50.

Salmon, G., Jones, S., & Armellini, A. (2008). Building institutional capability in e-learning design. *Research in Learning Technology, 16*(2), 95–109.

Schelly, C. L., Davies, P. L., & Spooner, C. L. (2011). Student perceptions of faculty implementation of universal design for learning. *Journal of Postsecondary Education and Disability, 24*(1), 17–30.

Shute, V. J. (2008). Focus on formative feedback. *Review of Educational Research, 78*(1), 153–89.

Smith, F. G. (2012). Analyzing a college course that adheres to the Universal Design for Learning (UDL) framework. *Journal of the Scholarship of Teaching and Learning, 12*(3), 31–61.

Statista. (2022). *Smartphone usage in the United Kingdom 2012–2020, by age.* Retrieved from *https://www.statista.com/statistics/300402/smartphone-usage-in-the-uk-by-age/*

Tait, H., Entwistle, N. J., & McCune, V. (1998). ASSIST: A reconceptualisation of the Approaches to Studying Inventory. In C. Rust (Ed.), *Improving learners as learners* (pp. 262–71). Oxford, UK: Oxford Brookes University.

Tobin, T. J., & Behling, K. T. (2018). *Reach everyone, teach everyone: Universal design for learning in higher education.* Morgantown, WV: West Virginia University Press.

Twenge, J. M. (2017). *iGen: Why today's super-connected kids are growing up less rebellious, more tolerant, less happy—and completely unprepared for adulthood. And what that means for the rest of us.* New York, NY: Simon and Schuster.

Tyng, C. M., Amin, H. U., Saad, M. N., & Malik, A. S. (2017). The influences of emotion on learning and memory. *Frontiers in Psychology*, 1454.

UNESCO. (2022). *Higher education global data report (Summary).* A contribution to the World Higher Education Conference 18–20 May 2022. Retrieved from *https://bangkok.unesco.org/content/unesco-higher-education-global-data-report*

Usher, J., MacNeill, S., & Creanor, L. (2018). Evolutions of Carpe Diem for learning design. *Compass: Journal of Learning and Teaching, 11*(1), 1–8.

Vermunt, J. D. (1998). The regulation of constructive learning processes. *British Journal of Educational Psychology, 68*(2), 149–71.

Weinstein, C. E., Palmer, D., & Schulte, A. C. (1987). *Learning and study strategies inventory (LASSI).* Clearwater, FL: H & H Publishing.

Wiggins, G., & McTighe, J. (2005). *Understanding by design.* Alexandria, VA: Association for Supervision and Curriculum Development.

Winter, R. (2003). Contextualising the patchwork text: Addressing problems of coursework assessment in higher education. *Innovations in Education and Teaching International, 40*(2), 112–22.

World Economic Forum. (2020). *Future of jobs report October 2020.* Retrieved from *http://www3.weforum.org/docs/WEF_Future_of_Jobs_2020.pdf*

Zeegers, P. (2001). Approaches to learning in science: A longitudinal study. *British Journal of Educational Psychology, 71*(1), 115–32.

# Index

## A

abstract conceptualization, 168
accessibility
    of materials/resources, 58–59, 62
    providing, 71
    of technology, 123–125, 127–135
    technology to enhance, 122
    as UDL value, 14, 65
action planning for teachers, 170–174
action/expression of learning
    in the Cheese Sandwich, 72
    means for/goals of, 10, 12
    *See also* demonstrated learning
active learning, 52, 58, 91, 148
activities, learning
    assessments aligned with, 102
    in the Cheese Sandwich, 56–58
    in CUTLAS design, 147–148, 152
    feedback during, 48
    goal-aligned, 91, 92
    goals of, 84
    as methods toward goals, 91
    overview of, 45–46
    practicing for, 92
    in Roadmap for Teaching, 41, 42
    teacher reflection on, 99
    variety in, 94, 97–98
affective network, 8
aims, teaching, 84
analysis
    in cognitive taxonomy, 36, 37, 38
    as goal of learning, 86
Anderson, L. W., 37, 38
anti-discrimination laws, 3
anxiety, 24
application
    in cognitive taxonomy, 36, 37, 38
    outcomes based on, 88

assessments
    activity/goal-aligned, 101–104
    of background knowledge, 20
    barriers via, 10–11
    vs. "evaluation," 105
    formative and summative, 102–103, 106
    as key component of effective learning, 19, 80
    learner needs for, 22–23
    of, for, and as learning, 105–109
    learning driven by, 79
    offering variable, 67
    in Roadmap for Teaching, 42
    self-assessments, 46
    of session-level learning, 85
    *See also* evaluation
assistive technology, 120–121
attention/commitment, 8–9, 93
attitudes, learner, 21–22
Ausubel, D, 39
autism, 21
"average learner," 17

## B

background knowledge, 71, 112
backward design, 44, 84, 142
barriers
    assessments as, 10–11
    cultural, 26
    digital poverty as, 124–125
    emotional, 24
    as environmental, 12–13, 67
    of fixed mindset, 14
    removing/reducing, 9–10, 26, 65–66, 120
    understanding potential, 5, 6, 21
belonging, 26
Black, Jodie, 122
blocks of learning, 41, 55, 85, 142

Bloom's taxonomy
    original and revised, 35–38
    outcomes based in, 88–89
    in Roadmap for Teaching, 41
blueprint, CUTLAS, 144
brain, the, 8
building, in CUTLAS, 151–152

## C

CAIeRO (Creating Aligned, Interactive, educational Resource Opportunities), 141–142
capability
    changing mindsets about, 13–14
    social/emotional factors, 24
    of teachers, 155–156
    as UDL value, 14
Carpe Diem methodology, 141
challenges
    mastery as, 175
    "missions" to address, 95, 116–117
    response to, 93
    in teaching, 155
    *See also* improvement
Cheese Sandwich approach
    access to materials in, 58–59
    customization in, 64, 66–68
    in CUTLAS design, 146–147, 150
    to design blocks of learning, 142
    effectiveness of, 74–75, 98
    evidence-informed, 68–72
    flipped learning in, 61–62
    hierarchy of skills in, 63–64
    learning factors in, 77–80
    peer/teacher support in, 57–58, 117
    principles of, 61
    Roadmap for Teaching via, 59–60
    self-direction in, 58
    time constraints and, 104
    topic coverage in, 55–57
    transferability in, 73–75
    UDL principles in, 64–66, 68–72
classes
    observation of, 162, 164
    recordings of, 120, 125
closed captioning, 130
cognition
    emotion and, 23
    metacognition, 7, 37, 38, 69, 74
cognitive skills
    active learning for, 45
    Cheese Sandwich to develop, 75
    hierarchy of, 35–38, 74
    mastering, 63
    passive learning of, 52
    practicing to develop, 39–40
    transferability of, 73
    *See also* higher-order thinking skills; lower-order thinking skills
collaboration, 58, 80, 144
commitment, 78–79, 93, 175
communication, 15
competence
    cultural, 27–28
    and group work, 23
    self-perceived, 21, 22
comprehension
    in cognitive taxonomy, 36
    "getting it," 79
    learner variability and, 17–18
    removing barriers to, 9
    varying materials for optimum, 10
conceptual knowledge, 37, 38
concrete experience, direct and indirect, 167
constructive alignment, 46, 102
constructivist approach
    and the Cheese Sandwich, 57
    defined, 39
    goals in, 78
    learning support via, 73
courses, 6
COVID-19 pandemic, 124
creating in cognitive taxonomy, 37, 38
cultural perspectives
    differences in, 18
    of learners, 25–27
    self-knowledge of your, 27–28
curiosity, 22
curriculum
    co-created, 22
    cultural relevance of, 25
    "higher" cognition in, 38
    as key component of effective learning, 19
    Meyer et al. model of, 42
customization
    of assessments, 105
    in the Cheese Sandwich, 64, 66–68
    enhanced learning via, 64
    iGen expectation of, 4–5, 122
    via technology, 122
    in UDL, 7, 12
CUTLAS (Creating Universal Teaching Learning and Assessment Strategies)

building in, 151–152
defining phase, 143–144
designing in, 144–151
four phases of, 142–143
methods behind, 141–142
overview of, 141, 142, 154
reviewing in, 153–154

## D

declarative knowledge, 92
deep/meaningful learning
    via higher-order thinking, 63
    as mastery, 38
    vs. rote learning, 36
    tasks supporting, 74
    teacher/peer support for, 62
    transferability of, 74
defining phase of CUTLAS, 143–144
delivery up approach, 142
demographic information, 20, 27
demonstrated learning
    via aligned assessments, 101
    anxiety and, 24
    forms of assessing, 102–103
    preferences and, 28
    variability in, 10–11
    as written goal, 86
description, 86
design, instructional
    backward, 44–45, 84
    barriers via, 10, 21, 24
    of the Cheese Sandwich, 59–60
    in CUTLAS, 141, 144–151
    effectiveness of, 16
    feedback in, 113
    key elements of, 139–141
    learner-centric, 13
    for learners in margins, 120–121
    neural networks and, 8
    to remove barriers, 66
    Roadmap for Teaching, 41–43
    time dedicated to, 15
    *See also* UDL (Universal Design for Learning)
design down approach, 142
diagnostic assessments, 20
didactic teaching, 9, 52, 58, 70, 71, 72
differentiation
    evaluation and, 46–47
    via formative assessment, 107
    social/emotional effects of, 23–24
"digesting" learning, 79

digital poverty, 124–125
disabilities, students with
    designing for, 120–121
    laws protecting, 3–4
disadvantages, assessments as, 10–11
diversity
    among students, 3–4, 53
    cultural differences, 18
    as UDL value, 14
doing, learning by, 79
dominant cultural group, 25–26
dyslexia, 17–18, 67

## E

EDUCARE? model, 96–99, 149, 150
education
    constant change in, 155
    learner-centric, 19, 29–31, 69
    self-directed, 22
    values critical to, 14
    *See also* higher education
educators. *See* teachers
effect size, 72
emotions, 23–25
engagement with learning
    in the Cheese Sandwich, 70
    via cultural relevance, 26
    factors affecting, 20–27
    feedback for, 48
    importance of, 78, 93
    means for/goals of, 8–9, 12
equitability, 14, 105, 175
errors, 93
evaluation
    vs. "assessment," 105
    in the Cheese Sandwich, 56
    in cognitive taxonomy, 36, 37, 38
    in CUTLAS design, 147, 152
    feedback after, 48
    frequency of, 113
    learning activities and, 95–96
    overview of activities for, 46–48
    of progress toward goals, 86
    in Roadmap for Teaching, 41, 42
    of teachers, 156–161, 172–173
    *See also* assessments
exams, 10–11, 23
exclusion, 5, 26
expectations, student, 4
experimentation, active, 168–170
Experiential Learning Cycle, 166, 167, 169

expert learners
  assessments for, 107
  characteristics of, 44, 83
  as goal-directed, 46
  mastery by, 38
  past examples of, 13
  self-knowledge of, 19, 94
  skills applied by, 35
  UDL to become, 7

## F

face validity, 158
factual knowledge, 37, 38
fairness, 105
feed forward, 106
feedback
  in the Cheese Sandwich, 57
  in CUTLAS design, 154
  effectiveness of, 73
  importance of, 79, 111
  learning via, 94–95, 107, 112
  medals/missions in, 95, 102, 116–117
  to modify understanding, 39
  qualitative, 102
  reception of, 114
  in Roadmap for Teaching, 41, 42, 48–49, 111
  on skills practiced, 98
  sources for, 118
  for/by teachers, 170
  timing of, 113, 114
  triangulated, 117–118
  *See also* mastery-oriented feedback
feedback cage, 118
feedback from learners
  in the Cheese Sandwich, 58
  on cultural factors, 26
  for defining in CUTLAS, 144
  iteration based on, 19, 66
  supported by teachers, 165
  teacher development via, 157–158
  UDL-based survey of, 158–161
feedback seekers, 118
feedback-corrected practice
  in the Cheese Sandwich, 59
  diagram of, 97, 113
  as learner-centric, 63–64
  via medals/missions, 95
  in Roadmap for Teaching, 48, 49
  as trial and error, 93
  understanding via, 39

flipped learning, 61–62
focus, 72
formative assessment, 102–103, 107
Freeman, Jonathan B., 18
functioning knowledge, 92

## G

"getting it," 79–80
goal-directed learning
  constructive alignment for, 102
  CUTLAS as, 141–142
  expert learners via, 83
  hierarchy of goals, 88–90
  outcome types in, 88
  and reception of feedback, 114
  session/unit/program outcomes, 84–85
  UDL as, 44, 83
  writing down your, 86–88
goals/outcomes
  activities aligned with, 45, 92
  assessments aligned with, 101, 104, 109
  clearly defined, 18–19, 78, 83, 84, 86–88
  in CUTLAS design, 146–147, 153
  evaluating mastery of, 46
  hierarchy of, 88–89
  learners' personal, 21–22
  levels of, 88–90
  of mastery, 7, 61
  and reception of feedback, 114
  in Roadmap for Teaching, 41, 42, 43–45
  session/unit/program, 84–85, 103
  in teaching action plans, 171
  technology to support, 126
  types of, 87, 88
  varied paths to, 7, 11, 66–67, 94
graphic organizer software, 121
group work
  differentiation and, 23–24
  gauging learner views on, 24–25
  as potential barrier, 9, 21

## H

habits, permanent, 39
Hattie, Professor John, 13, 18, 72, 83
higher education
  content focus in, 39–40
  enrollment statistics, 3
  "higher" cognition in, 38, 75
  technology in, 4–5
  traditional model of, 51–53, 67
  and UDL, 5–6

higher-order thinking skills
    active learning for, 45, 91
    applied to content, 43–44
    applying/developing, 40
    in Bloom's taxonomy, 35–38
    in the Cheese Sandwich, 55–57, 60
    as functioning knowledge, 92
    in learning goal hierarchy, 88–89
    lower-order as preceding, 63
    "making sense" of, 113
    mastery via, 38, 73
    self-directed learning of, 52
    teacher/peer support for, 62
hinge point for learning outcomes (Hattie), 73

## I

iGeneration
    learning expectations of, 4–5, 122
    smartphone access for, 125
    stereotypes about, 123
implementation, UDL, 5
improvement
    assessments for, 102
    via learner feedback, 18–19
    in teaching, 155
    UDL effectiveness via, 14
inclusion, 14, 175
independent work
    gauging learner views on, 24–25
    preference for, 9, 21
    self-assessments for, 108
information overload, 70, 71
interest
    learning about, 22–23
    recruiting, 8, 78
    supporting, 70
iteration
    effective teaching via, 14
    via feedback, 112
    learner variability and, 19
    time required for, 15

## K

Kennette, Lynne, 158
knowledge
    background, 20, 39, 40, 47, 71, 112
    in cognitive taxonomy, 36, 37
    declarative vs. functioning, 92
    outcomes based in, 88
    types of, 37

Kolb, David, 166
Krathwohl, D. R., 37, 38

## L

language, 9, 17–18
LD (learning disabilities), 121
learner variability
    examples of, 17–18
    how to assess, 139, 143
    multiple paths based on, 67
    technology benefits for, 120–121, 122
learners
    catering to, 74
    changing mindsets about, 13
    diversity of, 3–4
    as expert learners, 7
    feedback from. *See* feedback from learners
    as feedback seekers, 118
    getting to know your, 20–28, 140
    goal-directed, 44, 102
    iGen tech expectations, 4–5
    learner-centric teaching of, 19
    in the margins, 120–121
    means of engaging, 8–9
    strengths and needs of, 29–31
    surveying, 27
    UDL benefits to, 5–6, 12–13
    variable pathways for, 66–67, 123
learning
    assessment of/for/as, 105–109
    in the Cheese Sandwich, 55–57
    in cognitive skill hierarchy, 35–38
    factors influencing, 77–78
    feedback-supported, 48, 113–114
    goal-directed. *See* goal-directed learning
    practicing for, 63
    supports for, 72–73
    teacher- vs. learner-centric, 19, 51–53, 84
    for teachers, 155
    as test of teachers, 15–16
    transferability of, 73–74
    varied paths for, 120–121, 123–125
    *See also* activities, learning
learning needs
    diversity of, 3–4, 53
    evaluation of, 47
    importance of meeting, 5
    interest and, 22–23
    mindset changes on, 13
    social/emotional factors, 23–25
    UDL to meet, 5, 14–15

understanding, 29–31, 108
variability in, 7–12, 17–18, 97–98
lectures, 9, 52
legal issues, 3
lower-order thinking skills
    in Bloom's taxonomy, 35–37
    in the Cheese Sandwich, 40, 55–57, 60
    as declarative knowledge, 92
    in learning goal hierarchy, 88–89
    as preceding higher-order, 63
    in self-directed study, 62

## M

"making sense," 79–80, 113
margins, learners in the, 120–121
mastery
    via active learning, 91
    in Bloom's taxonomy, 38
    defined, 175
    different "paths" to, 53, 67
    via EDUCARE? model, 96–99
    feedback and, 42–43
    via higher-order thinking, 62, 92
    as learning goal, 43–45, 61
    of lower- vs higher-order skills, 35
    of low-tech teaching, 119
    means of achieving, 7–8
    UDL principles for, 68–69
mastery-oriented feedback
    characteristics of, 114–115
    importance of, 69
    during learning activities, 48
    for skills practice, 39
materials/resources
    accessibility of, 58–59, 62
    in CUTLAS design, 148–151, 152
    multimedia, 61
    review/update of, 16
    in Roadmap for Teaching, 42
    for self-directed study, 58
    for teaching goals, 172
    in the UDL framework, 64–66
    use of varied, 9–10, 15
medals/missions in feedback, 95, 102, 115–116
mentors/role models, 27
metacognition, 7, 37, 38, 69, 74
methods of teaching
    in the Cheese Sandwich, 56–57
    CUTLAS, 141–142
    in EDUCARE? model, 96–99
    learner-customized, 13
    most effective, 73
    offering variable, 66–67, 87–88
    Ripples on a Pond, 77, 78, 113
    in Roadmap for Teaching, 42
    student-centric, 16
    traditional, teacher-centric, 51–52
mindset
    learners' personal, 21–22
    UDL, 13–14
missions in feedback, 95, 116–117
mobile devices, 4–5, 125
modules
    aims/objectives in, 84
    with CUTLAS design, 142
    defined, 6
    module-level outcomes, 84–85
Moore, Eric, 122
motivation
    feedback for, 48
    importance of, 78
    learners' personal, 21–22
    supporting, 93
multimedia resources, 61, 65

## N

needing to learn, 78–79
neural networks, 8
Novak, Katie, 5, 20

## O

objectives, teaching, 84
observation, of teachers, 162–164, 167
Ontario Ministry of Education, 31
open book exams, 11
options, providing, 9
outcomes. *See* goals/outcomes

## P

participation, 72
passive learning, 52, 67, 92
    *See also* didactic teaching
patchwork-style assessment, 102–103, 106
patience for attaining mastery, 175
PDF files, 133–135
peers
    anxiety in front of, 24
    in the Cheese Sandwich, 56–58
    feedback for/from, 117
    peer reviews, 108
    support from, 24–25
    teacher peer reviews, 157, 162–166

Peer-Supported Review (P-SR), 162–163
performance of learning, 106
permanence, 39
persistence, supporting, 8
personalization
    iGen expectation of, 4–5
    in UDL, 7, 12
Petty, Geoff, 63, 95, 96, 170
podcasts, 125, 131–132
poverty, digital, 124–125
PowerPoint slides, 65, 127–129
practicing skills
    EDUCARE? model for, 96–99
    feedback for, 48–49
    of higher-order thought, 89–90, 92
    learning via, 63, 79
    mastery via, 95
    of teaching, 175
    as trial and error, 93
    until permanent, 39–40
    *See also* feedback-corrected practice
preferences
    learning needs and, 22
    peer vs. independent work, 24–25
    surveys for learner, 27
    UDL for understanding, 5
procedural knowledge, 37, 38
professional development, 4
programs (degrees), 6, 84

## R

Race, Phil, 21, 77, 79, 80, 113
racial issues, 26
reading alternatives, 9–10
"reading" for a degree, 52
recognition network, 8, 9
recordings, 120, 125
reflection
    about your values, 14
    on educational design, 74
    on learning outcomes, 90
    teacher self-reflection, 166–170
    on teaching mindset, 13
remembering in cognitive taxonomy, 37, 38
representation, 9–10, 12, 71
resources. *See* materials/resources
reverse effects, 18
reviews
    in CUTLAS design, 153–154
    student peer reviews, 108
    teacher peer reviews, 162–166

Ripples on a Pond method, 77, 78, 113
Roadmap for Teaching
    action/goal/evaluation in, 101
    Cheese Sandwich and, 59–60, 98–99
    in CUTLAS design, 144, 145, 148
    feedback in, 79, 111, 114
    in instructional design, 139, 140
    outcomes in, 114
    overview of, 41–49
    technology and, 126
rote/surface learning, 36, 74

## S

safety of learning environment, 14
screencasts, 125
self-assessments, 40, 108, 117
self-directed learning
    in the Cheese Sandwich, 56, 58
    feedback on, 118
    in higher education, 22
    materials for, 61–62
    time constraints and, 104
    in traditional education models, 52
self-evaluation, 116, 117, 166
self-knowledge
    cultural, 27–28
    in expert learners, 19
    via self-assessments, 108
self-regulation, 8
seminars, 52
sessions, 57, 85
sharing, 58
skills
    hierarchy of cognitive, 35–38
    for learning, 8
    need for lifelong, 4, 74, 155
    outcomes based in, 88
    practice for mastery of, 39–40
smartphone access, 125
social justice, 14
social/emotional factors, 23–25
software, 120, 121
status quo, limitations of, 51–53
storyboard, CUTLAS, 145–146, 149
strategic network, 8, 10
strengths, learner, 29–31, 102
students. *See* learners
styles, learning
    self-knowledge of your, 8
    surveying for, 27–28
    variability in, 9, 12, 13

summative assessment, 102–103, 106, 113
support
    "getting it" via, 79–80
    for motivation, 93
    teacher/peer, 24–25, 56–58, 62
    for technologies used, 123
    technology as, 120–121, 126
Surface, Deep, and Transfer learning model, 40, 73
surveys, 27
synchronous learning, 125
synthesis in Bloom's taxonomy, 36, 37

## T

teachers
    action planning for, 170–174
    benefits of technology to, 122–123
    changing mindsets of, 13
    in the Cheese Sandwich, 56–58
    constant learning for, 155–156
    evaluation of, 156–161
    feedback for/by, 170
    feedback from, 48–49
    habits of effective, 14
    influence on students, 23–24
    mastery support by, 69
    observation of, 162–164
    peer reviews by/for, 162–166
    self-reflection by, 166–170
    traditional role of, 51–52
    UDL for, 5–6
    values examined by, 14–15
teaching
    activities, in CUTLAS, 148
    aligned with assessment, 103
    learner-centered, 19
    mastery of low-tech, 119
    time constraints, 104
    units of, 6
technology
    access to, 123–125, 127–135
    assumptions about, 123–124
    benefits of, 122–123
    Carpe Diem method with, 141
    iGen expectations for, 4–5, 122
    for learners in margins, 120–121
    over-use of, 119
    purpose of using, 126
    UDL delivery via, 119
    workforce changes via, 4
thinking. *See* cognition

time considerations
    feedback timing, 113, 114
    in learning UDL, 15–16
    teaching time constraints, 104
transcripts, 130, 131
transferability
    in the Cheese Sandwich, 56–57, 60, 73–75, 78
    emphasizing, 40
triangulated feedback, 117–118
Twenge, Professor Jean, 4

## U

UDL (Universal Design for Learning)
    barriers reduced via, 26
    defined, 5
    designing via, 139, 141
    effectiveness of, 73
    as goal-directed, 44, 83
    Guidelines, 11, 39, 43
    higher education and, 5–6
    learning pathways in, 67
    mindset of, 13–14
    practice of, 14, 15–16
    technology in, 119, 122
    three principles of, 7–12
    time commitment to, 15–16
    timeliness of, 3, 53
UDL Navigators in Higher Education (Black and Moore), 122
UDL principles
    assessment within, 105
    via the Cheese Sandwich, 64–66, 68–72
    in CUTLAS design, 146
    evaluations aligned with, 46, 47
    guidelines for, 43
    layering on, 64–66
    learner interest and, 22
    learner survey based on, 158
    and learner-specific surveys, 29
    low-tech mastery of, 119
    overview of, 7–12
    practicing/mastering, 175–176
understanding
    in cognitive taxonomy, 37, 38
    demonstrations of, 101–109
    via feedback, 112
    measuring, 86
    modification of, 39
    teacher support for, 62
units, 6, 84–85, 142

## V

values
    cultural, 26
    examining your, 14–15, 16
variability
    among learners, 3–4, 17, 53
    in brain networks, 8
    changing sources of, 66
    in learning activities, 46, 94
    in learning materials, 58–59
    of means in EDUCARE? 97–98
    planning for, 20
    in why/what/how of learning, 7–12
VARK questionnaire, 28
verbalizing learning, 80
videos, 65, 129–131
Visible Learning for Teachers (Hattie), 18, 72, 83

## W

Wilson, Nathan, 158
Word documents, 132–133
word processing, 11
writing assists, 120–121

# Acknowledgments

The writing of this book would not have been possible without the inspiration, ideas, and support, not to mention kindness, of a plethora of colleagues from across the United Kingdom, Ireland, the United States, and Canada.

I would like to personally thank all of those people working for various colleges, universities, and other charitable and not-for-profit organizations who gave their time to talk with me about effective learning and teaching in the general sense, and Universal Design for Learning more specifically.

This book is the product of the wisdom shared by those who inspired me to change my perspective on what effective teaching is, as well as to continually try to be the best teacher I can be, instilling in me a love for teaching that grows stronger with each passing year. This book is also the product of the wisdom shared by those who live and breathe UDL. Without your support and generosity, I would never have been able to understand what UDL means, why it's important, and how it can be applied. Your stories, advice, and guidance form the core of this book.

I am especially grateful to the following people for either inspiring me, sharing their ideas with me, or giving me a platform to share the ideas that eventually became this book. Some have influenced this work without knowing it, while others will recognize their contribution more readily. Either way, if our paths had never crossed, this book would never have happened: Gill McInnes, Bev Alesbrook, Sue Morrison, Sally Olohan, Sara Baldwin, Tony Churchill, Abigail Moriarty, Angela O'Sullivan, Phil Scarrfe, Tina Sharpe, Geoff Petty, Alan Mortiboys, Phil Race, David Carless, Fiona Macneil, Dan Axson, Eric Moore, Katie Novak, Tesha Fritzgerald, Steve Nordmark, Olive Byrne, James Northridge, Dara Ryder, David Gordon, and Rachel Monaghan.

# About the Author

KEVIN L. MERRY, PhD, is the head of academic development and an associate professor of Learning, Teaching and Assessment at De Montfort University (DMU) in Leicester, United Kingdom. In his role, Kevin supports the adoption and application of Universal Design for Learning (UDL) among the university's large community of academic and professional services staff. He supports curriculum and instructional design, provides professional development and training, and develops resources and materials to support UDL implementation at DMU. An award-winning teacher, Kevin has received accolades for his approaches to accessible and inclusive curriculum design, and has become internationally renowned for his work on UDL. Through his role as founder and chair of the UDL United Kingdom and Ireland Higher Education Network (UDL-UKI), Kevin has supported adoption and implementation of UDL at higher education institutions in Europe, North America, and Asia. The purpose of the UDL-UKI network is to identify, promote, and support the development of approaches, models, tools, and practices that enable effective UDL practice in higher education settings.

# MORE FROM CAST

CAST is a nonprofit education research and development organization that created the Universal Design for Learning framework and UDL Guidelines. Our mission is to transform education design and practice until learning has no limits.

CAST supports learners and educators at every level through a variety of offerings:

- Innovative professional development
- Accessibility and inclusive technology resources
- Research, design, and development of inclusive and effective solutions
- Credentials for Universal Design for Learning
- And much more

Visit *www.cast.org* to learn more.